THE

# Berghoff Café

**COOKBOOK**

**OTHER BOOKS BY CARLYN BERGHOFF
WITH NANCY ROSS RYAN**

*The Berghoff Family Cookbook: From Our Table to
Yours, Celebrating a Century of Entertaining*

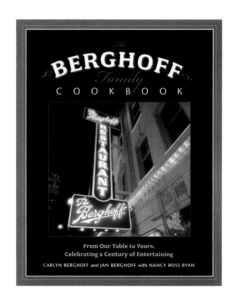

# THE
# Berghoff Café
## COOKBOOK

*Berghoff Family Recipes for Simple, Satisfying Food*

Carlyn Berghoff with Nancy Ross Ryan

Foreword by Rick Rodgers

Photography by Ally Gruener

**Andrews McMeel**
**Publishing, LLC**
Kansas City • Sydney • London

09 10 11 12 13 SDB 10 9 8 7 6 5 4 3 2 1

ISBN-13: 978-0-7407-8514-6
ISBN-10: 0-7407-8514-1

Library of Congress Control Number: 2009005571

Designer: Diane Marsh
Food Stylist: Susie Skoog
Photo courtesy of Carlyn Berghoff: xiv

www.andrewsmcmeel.com

## Thanks to my family:

My husband Jim McClure and my children Lindsey,
Sarah, and Todd, for their love and support

Great-grandfather Herman Joseph Berghoff,
for being an inspiration to us all

Grandfather Lewis Windthorst ("Todd") Berghoff,
for taking the helm and steering the Berghoff

Grandmother Carlyn, for her name and her incredible cooking

Great-aunt Vita, for warm memories and
her meringue surprise cookies

Uncle Clement Anthony Berghoff, for making the Berghoff bigger

My father and mother, Herman and Jan
Berghoff, for making the Berghoff great

My sister Julie and my brothers Pete and
Tim, for our childhood together

—Carlyn Berghoff McClure

# ❊ Contents ❊

*Acknowledgments* **ix**

*Foreword by Rick Rodgers* **xi**

*A Corned Beef Sandwich and . . .* **xiii**

Bar Snacks: Food for Drink     **1**

Soups: Big Bowls     **21**

Sandwiches: Something of Substance     **37**

Salads: To Make the Meal     **59**

Sides: Scene Stealers     **81**

Berghoff Plates: Daily Specials     **101**

Café Pizzas: A New Tradition     **117**

Desserts: Yesterday and Today     **131**

*Metric Conversions and Equivalents* **150**

*Index* **151**

# Acknowledgments

In writing this cookbook, I had the help, support, and guidance of a tremendously talented team:

Lisa Ekus-Saffer, friend and agent; Jean Lucas, Kirsty Melville, and Tim Lynch, keen editor, wise publisher, and expert art director at Andrews McMeel; Blake Swihart and Kathleen Sanderson, friends and recipe architects, Foodservice Solutions; Matt Reichel, executive chef; Enrique Sta Marie ("Bong") and Encarnacion Reynozo ("Chon"), restaurant and catering pastry chefs. These three key members of the Berghoff Group culinary team spent countless hours with me in my kitchen and theirs testing recipes; Ashley Perich, my assistant, who spent just as many hours on the computer on the book's behalf; photographer Ally Gruener and her crew: assistant Alyssa Pazdan, digital technicians Brian Eaves and Anthony Tortoriello, lighting technician David Moenkhaus, and prop stylist Carey Thorton; food stylist Susie Skoog; Hall's Rental Services, Inc., and BBJ Linen Rentals for the generous use of props and linens; Nancy Ross Ryan, friend and writer.

Everyone should be so lucky to have this team.

—Carlyn Berghoff

# Foreword

BY RICK RODGERS

I'm not from Chicago, but I consider the Berghoff Café a home away from home. Whenever I travel to the Windy City, I make a beeline to the corner of State and Adams, where I know that a substantial and tasty meal awaits me. In my case, it is literally food just like Grandma used to make, as both the Berghoffs and I share a Germanic heritage. Serve me a golden-brown, crispy schnitzel with a plate of buttery spaetzle on the side and a tall, foamy glass of ice-cold Berghoff beer, and I am your willing slave.

I first met Carlyn Berghoff, who would also become one of Chicago's most respected caterers, over twenty years ago at a catering conference, when neither of us dreamed that we would ever write a cookbook. In *The Berghoff Café Cookbook*, she has collected the menu items that make it so difficult for me to choose what to order whenever I visit her restaurant. You will have the same dilemma deciding what to cook from this book. For a taste of old Chicago, you might make a meal of Beer-Braised Pork Loin, Lyonnaise Potatoes (the Berghoff Café's potato dishes are renowned), bacony Green Beans, and Walnut-Applesauce Coffee Cake for dessert. Or, to experience some of the new dishes that Carlyn

has added to the traditional fare, cook up one of the pizza or panini recipes, many of which use "big-shouldered" Chicago flavors like corned beef (the world's best?), sauerkraut, and smoked sausages. Talk about the best of both worlds!

Throughout the book, acting as a kind of seasoning, you will find fascinating historical tidbits about the recipes. Reading some of these factoids, I got very nostalgic for Chicago, particularly for the Berghoff Café. To boost my spirits, I went into my kitchen and baked a batch of The Chip Cookie with milk chocolate chips. It wasn't quite the same as being there, but until my next trip it will more than suffice.

# A Corned Beef Sandwich and...

It all started, more than one hundred years ago, with a corned beef sandwich, a stein of Berghoff beer, and a pickle. It helps to remember this when I'm running up and down four flights of stairs in the century-old Berghoff building in Chicago—the same stairs that my great-grandfather, my grandfather, and my mom and dad used.

I wrote this book for my great-grandfather Herman Joseph Berghoff, and for his simple, satisfying Berghoff Café food, which is our foundation. I'm the fourth generation to work in Chicago's Berghoff building (home of the famous Berghoff restaurant that he founded), and to continue his tradition.

Whenever I hit a rough patch in the restaurant business (and in life), I think of him. I came to the restaurant business as a chef, after graduating from the Culinary Institute of America. He went from immigrant to brewer to restaurateur.

When he was seventeen he left his home in Dortmund, Germany, and

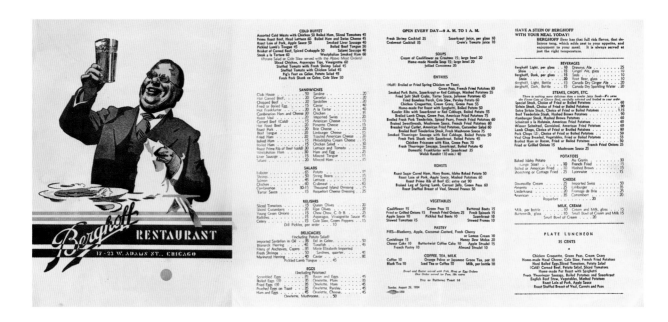

boarded a ship for America. When I was seventeen I was in my last year in high school and getting ready to go to chef's school. Great-grandad landed in Brooklyn with almost no money, and he quickly lost what he had to a con artist. He worked on a sugar plantation, for Buffalo Bill in his Wild West Show (Great-grandad had read about the Wild West in Germany and frontiersmen were his heroes), on the railroads and aboard a ship. However, barely twelve years after he landed in America, he had his own brewery.

## The Berghoff Café Then

Great-grandfather wasn't a chef, but he opened the Berghoff Café in 1898 in Chicago because the city wouldn't give him a license to wholesale his beer to restaurants and hotels. Thirty local breweries were supplying the city, and Herman's brewery was in Indiana. That made him an out-of-towner.

Great-grandad was a born entrepreneur who brought three of his brothers to America, became an American citizen in 1876, got married, had kids, and by 1882 opened his own brewery in Fort Wayne, Indiana. He certainly wasn't going to let a wholesale license stand between him and his beer. So in 1898 he got a retail restaurant license and opened the Berghoff Café at State and Adams streets, where he sold his own beer at a nickel a glass and ten cents a stein. Why he named it Berghoff Café instead of Berghoff Saloon remains a mystery, because it had a long mahogany bar with a brass rail, spittoons, and stools. I suspect he called it a café because it was located in the middle of the downtown shopping district dominated by department stores patronized by women. Great-grandfather was shrewd enough to realize that *café* sounded more genteel than *saloon*, even though he wasn't counting on women as customers. (The Berghoff was for men only, and Herman's vow that "ladies will not be seated at the bar" was not broken until 1969, when it was integrated by a delegation of four women from NOW—the National Organization for Women.)

## The Free Lunch

To build business he offered the proverbial free lunch with a ten-cent stein. For the free lunch, the big spenders had their choice of three sandwiches: corned beef, boiled ham, or a real frankfurter, plump and flavorful with a natural casing that gave a satisfying "pop!" when your teeth sank in. Each sandwich came with a hard-boiled egg and a fat, juicy dill pickle.

Great-grandfather Herman had a knack for satisfying customers' appetites for food and drink. In addition to his light and dark Berghoff beers, he also sold his own blended whiskey.

## Time to Move

In 1913, fifteen years after he opened the café, the building it occupied at State and Adams was scheduled for demolition so a high-rise could be built. So Great-grandad moved the Berghoff a short distance west on the same block of Adams to the three-story Stone building, named for its original owner, Horatio O. Stone, one of Chicago's pioneers and a real estate developer.

And by 1914 business was so good that the free lunch was only a memory. Our family's first surviving printed menu dates from 1914 and shows that café food had expanded to include relishes, soups, eggs and omelets, potatoes and vegetables, cheeses, ready-to-serve entrées, sausages, and steaks and chops to order. Cold meat platters were very popular and they came with potato salad. The sandwich section listed twenty-nine varieties. The food was simple and satisfying, and the original three sandwiches were still on the menu—but no longer free. The corned beef and boiled ham cost 15 cents apiece, and the frankfurter cost 20 cents.

## From Café to Restaurant

The big change in the café menu happened because of Prohibition. In 1920 Prohibition became law and Herman was legally obliged to stop brewing and selling beer. Determined as ever, he started brewing and serving his own line of Bergo soda pops: root beer, orange tang, and more, and the legal near beer (0.5 percent alcohol). He expanded the menu, added table service, and turned the café into a full-service restaurant. And the rest, as they say, is history. His sons Lewis (my grandfather) and Clement joined him, and by the time Prohibition ended in 1933, they were well on their way to making the Berghoff one of the most famous restaurants in Chicago.

In 1936 the restaurant expanded to another storefront right next door in the Stone building. And in 1950 the restaurant expanded west again into the adjoining four-story Palmer building. Like the Stone building, it was named for its original owner, Potter Palmer, Chicago's "merchant prince." Today those two joined buildings, called the Berghoff Building, house the Berghoff Group: catering, bar, restaurant, and café.

## The Café Today

The café food, which was Great-grandfather's heart and soul, always remained with us through generations of Berghoffs and the growth of the menu and the restaurant. He still came to his restaurant every day—until the day he died in December 1934.

The café food and drink he created—the Berghoff foundation—is simple and satisfying, nothing fancy, and not at all fussy. And you can still enjoy this same kind of food today at the Berghoff Café. One café is located on Adams

Street, downstairs from the restaurant, and the second café is located at O'Hare airport. Many of the café's menu items are served at the bar and also at lunch in the restaurant.

## Reuse, Recycle, Reinvent

Our café food is built upon three principles that work in the restaurant as well as at my home: reuse, recycle, and reinvent. Our ingredients, like the ingredients I use at home, are basic and simple—so simple that you might wonder how we can make such a varied menu with so many different daily and weekly specials from so few ingredients.

We reuse our basics, get great mileage from them, and waste nothing. So potatoes become Mashed Potatoes, Lyonnaise Potatoes, hash browns, Potato Salad, oven-roasted potatoes, potato pancakes, New Potato Salad with Dill, french fries, cottage fries, and Smoked Sausage and Potato Pizza, to name just a few of the dishes they star in.

We also recycle perfectly wholesome cooked foods. Roasted Herb-Marinated Turkey Breast stars in the Turkey Reuben, but there's enough left for Turkey, Okra, and Rice Soup, turkey salads, turkey à la king, turkey croquettes, sub sandwich, hot turkey and mashed potato sandwich with gravy, turkey and Swiss cheese panini . . . and we even shred it and mix it with sauce for a BBQ sandwich.

Plato said, "Necessity is the mother of invention." I say necessity is the mother of reinvention. At the café and at my home, that is certainly true. If I thought restaurant customers got tired of some of the same dishes fast, and always wanted something new and different, well, that was before I had kids. The Berghoff Café pizzas are great examples of how we reinvent dishes (while reusing and recycling ingredients). Pizza is a familiar dish in America and its ingredients are pretty standard: crust, red sauce, cheese and meats, and/or vegetables. The Berghoff Café pizzas are different. Our crusts have added seasonings and herbs: Caraway Crust has caraway seeds, and Herb Crust has oregano, basil, and rosemary. There's not a drop of red sauce on our crusts. Instead we spread them with olive oil and mustard, or olive oil and garlic for added crispness and flavor. And we top them with signature ingredients: Four-Cheese Pizza with Herb Crust; Brat, Kraut, and Swiss Cheese Pizza with Caraway Crust; Smoked Sausage and Potato Pizza with Caraway Crust; Onion and Bacon Pizza with Caraway or Pepper Crust; and Veggie Pizza with Herb Crust.

Even the chocolate chip cookie has been reinvented at the café. It's now The Chip Cookie. You can vary the chip you use or you can divide the dough in three and add three different chips. At home, I am constantly reinventing familiar dishes for my family, in café style. Instead of salad, I give them a salad bar: individual bowls of greens and an assortment of chopped vegetables plus shredded cheese to top them with. Instead of a bowl of potato chips, I put the chips inside the sandwich for portion control and extra crunch. Leftover meats, vegetables, cheese—you name it, a sandwich becomes a panini.

## Tradition with a Twist

Café food is not only very basic, it's very traditional, some would say old-fashioned: relish trays, soft pretzels, Thuringer sausages, rye bread, and mashed potatoes. Traditional food is very tasty, but if it's prepared the way my grandmother Carlyn cooked it, it is also very labor intensive and often high in fat. I like the flavors and the simplicity, but not the work and the calories. So when I give tradition a twist—in the café and at home—I keep the flavors but decrease the work and calories, and I often update the dish for today's tastes. For example, to my grandmother's relish tray I have added a Green Onion Dip. When grandmother Carlyn made mashed potatoes, she would peel and boil the potatoes in water, drain them, put them through a ricer, then whip them with butter and cream. Delicious. My twist on tradition is to cook the potatoes until tender in chicken or vegetable broth, drain them but save the broth, mash them in the same pan with a potato masher, then whip them with some of the cooking stock and add just a little butter. Just as yummy, but half the fat and half the work.

## The Café Recipes

The recipes in this cookbook represent the full range of Berghoff Café food. There are recipes from Great-grandfather Herman's café, updated for today's cook—I call these "tradition with a twist." For example, his beloved bratwurst sausages, served with sauerkraut and brown mustard, have become today's Sausage Wellingtons, a bratwurst baked in a brown mustard–brushed pastry crust. It can be eaten as a sandwich (with or without a side of sauerkraut), or sliced into segments and served as an hors d'oeuvre. The soft pretzels of yesterday become today's Soft Pretzels with five variations: Cheese, Caraway, Chocolate Chip, Cinnamon-Raisin, and Mini. The plain, cheese,

and caraway versions are topped with coarse salt, but the chocolate chip and cinnamon raisin pretzels are dusted with confectioners' sugar.

And this book features a selection from today's café menu of our customers' very favorite soups, salads, sandwiches, pizzas, and desserts. Our Berghoff Café pizzas are signatures, but so are our café salads: Shrimp Salad with Thousand Island Dressing, Asian Chicken Salad, Pear Salad with Greens, Candied Walnuts and Sun-Dried Cherries and, of course, Iceberg Wedge with Roquefort Dressing and Bacon.

Soups include the famous Berghoff Chili con Carne (that you can make with beef, pork, chicken, or turkey), Café Manhattan Clam Chowder, and Alsatian Onion Soup, a twist on traditional French onion soup.

The All-Day, All-Night Fried Egg Sandwich was good one hundred years ago for breakfast,

lunch, dinner, and supper—and it still is. Our Hamburger with Beer-Braised Onions is a customers' favorite, and the Real Thing Frankfurter sandwich may change your idea of hot dogs forever.

Desserts bring back the easy flavorful coffee cakes: Cream Cheese–Almond Coffee Cake and Walnut-Applesauce Coffee Cake. My twist on traditional apple pie is Apple Pie Squares with Cheddar Crust. And there's nothing else like Berghoff Bourbon-Prune Bread Pudding.

The recipes you'll find in this book are easy to prepare, look delicious on the plate, and are so good to eat. I think Great-grandfather Herman would be happy to know that 110 years later customers can still order a stein of Berghoff beer, a corned beef sandwich, and a pickle at the Berghoff Café. And if you really want the egg to go with it, we'll hard-boil one for you.

Cheers!

*Carlyn A Berghoff*

# CHAPTER 1

# BAR SNACKS

# Food for Drink

For the past 110 years, people have been eating while drinking at the Berghoff bar. It all started at Herman Berghoff's Berghoff Café in 1898, and it's still going on today. Food to go with drink isn't like an appetizer before dinner. It's more like an ongoing snack, something to keep nibbling on.

There are other requirements for good bar food. It has to have great flavors, and some of it at least, has to have enough texture to be noisy. Ever try to bite quietly into crisp celery, or chew silently on crunchy nuts?

Some of the recipes in this chapter are a blast from the past—Stuffed Celery, Sausage Wellingtons (yesterday's pigs in a blanket), and the Berghoff Relish Tray with today's onion dip. Our Deviled Eggs are an update of a '50s favorite. The Berghoff Nachos are new, only about fifteen years old, and the Soft Pretzels are older than Great-grandfather himself, but baked fresh daily.

Pretzels were a familiar food in Germany, Herman's birthplace, and in

1

Europe generally (see page 18). And they play a major role in Berghoff history. Herman came to this country in 1870. In 1872, he brought over his brother Henry. They were riding on a train passing through Fort Wayne, Indiana, in 1874, when the train stopped. Henry got off to buy some pretzels at a general store and the shopkeeper offered him a job, apparently too good to refuse. So he got back on the train, grabbed the luggage and his brother, and they both worked and settled in Fort Wayne. By 1882, Herman had his own brewery there. I like to think he'd be pleased to know that Berghoff beer and fresh pretzels are being served today in the Berghoff bar—and even more pleased to think

that Berghoff beer is being enjoyed in homes along with a fresh-baked pretzel.

Some of our recipes for bar food, such as Berghoff Nachos and Sausage Wellingtons, would make a great lunch. And you can create a complete tailgate or cocktail party menu by choosing your favorite five. For a sporting event–theme party, I would serve Candied Peanuts, Berghoff Nachos, Berghoff Relish Tray with Green Onion Dip, Bacon Pretzels, and Horseradish Deviled Eggs. For a cocktail party, try Sweet Asian Peanuts, Crab-Stuffed Celery, Caper Deviled Eggs, Sausage Wellingtons (sliced small), and mini, half-size Chocolate Chip Pretzels.

# Deviled Eggs with Three Fillings

**Makes 1½ cups filling, enough for 24 deviled egg halves**

*Technically speaking a "deviled" egg has a hot spice in the filling, such as cayenne or hot red pepper sauce. Berghoff Horseradish Deviled Eggs would certainly qualify. But the term has also become generic for stuffed eggs, and we make two popular versions for people who prefer a milder flavor. I serve these at home for appetizers, brunch, lunch, and dinner.*

*Use deviled egg fillings as a spread for panini, as a topping for open-faced hors d'oeuvre toast triangles, or as a dip for crudités.*

## CAPER DEVILED EGGS

12 hard-boiled eggs, peeled, halved lengthwise

¼ cup mayonnaise

3 tablespoons sour cream

1 tablespoon fresh lemon juice

1 teaspoon mustard powder

¼ cup minced green onion

2 tablespoons minced capers

2 teaspoons minced fresh parsley

Kosher salt and freshly ground black pepper

Whole capers, drained, for garnish

Separate the hard-boiled yolks from the egg white halves and place the yolks in the work bowl of a food processor fitted with the steel blade. Add the mayonnaise, sour cream, lemon juice, and mustard. Process until smooth. Transfer the mixture to a small bowl and stir in the green onion, minced capers, and parsley. Season with salt and pepper. Cover and refrigerate for 1 hour before using.

To fill, trim a thin slice from the bottom of a cooked egg white half so it stands level. Either spoon 1 tablespoon of filling into each egg cavity, smoothing the top, or transfer the filling to a pastry bag fitted with a ¼-inch plain tip and pipe the filling in. Garnish each egg with 1 to 3 drained capers.

## SMOKED SALMON DEVILED EGGS

12 hard-boiled eggs, peeled, halved lengthwise

1 tablespoon extra-virgin olive oil

1 tablespoon fresh lemon juice

1 tablespoon Dijon mustard

¼ cup mayonnaise

¼ cup minced smoked salmon

1½ tablespoons minced green onion

Freshly ground black pepper

Pinch of salt

Paper-thin slices green onion, for garnish

Separate the hard-boiled yolks from the egg white halves and place the yolks in the work bowl of a food processor fitted with the steel blade. Add the oil, lemon juice, mustard, and mayonnaise, and process until smooth. Add the salmon and pulse until smooth but not puréed. Transfer the mixture to a small bowl and stir in the minced green onion, pepper, and salt. Cover and chill for 1 hour before using.

To fill, trim a thin slice from the bottom of a cooked egg white half so it stands level. Either spoon 1 tablespoon of the filling into each egg cavity, smoothing the top, or transfer the filling to a pastry bag fitted with a ¼-inch plain tip and pipe the filling in. Garnish each egg with 1 or 2 slices of green onion.

## SHOT AND A WASH

Today's "shot and a wash"—not to be confused with a boilermaker—has a long history. A true boilermaker is a whiskey-filled shot glass dropped into a glass of beer, causing the beer to foam up and requiring the drinker to drink fast. Showoffs drink the beer and catch the shot glass between their lips. At the Berghoff bar we discourage guzzling and encourage responsible drinking. Our version of a shot and a wash is a stein of your choice of Berghoff beer with a shot of our fine seven-year-old Berghoff bourbon—a combination sure to please. According to Bob Skilnik, author of *Beer: A History of Brewing in Chicago*, in previous centuries water was often impure and one drank at one's peril. Beer, however, was a good alternative because at a certain point in brewing the product was boiled, thus purifying the beverage. But those taverns of yore also sold hard whiskey. Unfortunately, for centuries, distillation was very primitive, leaving all kinds of impurities in the whiskey along with a dreadful taste. So when a man drank a shot, how could he safely wash the taste out of his mouth? Not with water, but with beer.

## HORSERADISH DEVILED EGGS

12 hard-boiled eggs, peeled,
halved lengthwise

¼ cup mayonnaise

2 tablespoons prepared horseradish

1 tablespoon sweet pickle
juice (from pickle jar)

¼ teaspoon salt

¼ teaspoon freshly ground black pepper

24 fresh parsley leaves, for garnish

Separate the hard-boiled yolks from the egg white halves and place the yolks in the work bowl of a food processor fitted with the steel blade. Add the mayonnaise, horseradish, pickle juice, salt, and pepper, and process until smooth. Taste and add more horseradish if desired. Transfer the filling to a small bowl, cover, and refrigerate for 1 hour before using.

To fill, trim a thin slice from the bottom of a cooked egg white half so it stands level. Either spoon 1 tablespoon of filling into each egg cavity, smoothing the top, or transfer the filling to a pastry bag fitted with a ¼-inch plain tip and pipe the filling in. Garnish each egg with a parsley leaf.

*Note:* To hard-boil eggs, place the eggs in a large saucepan and cover with cold water by 1 inch. Cover the pot and bring to a rapid boil. Remove the pot from the heat and let stand, covered, for 10 minutes. Drain, crack the eggs against a flat surface in several places, cover with cold water, and let cool to room temperature. When cold, peel and halve lengthwise.

I usually cook fourteen eggs to allow for a couple of mishaps, such as eggs that don't peel well and/or tear.

# Berghoff Nachos

**Serves 8/Makes three 10-inch plates of nachos**

*Many Berghoff customers believe no beer is complete without Berghoff Nachos. Ours are special, made with Berghoff Chili con Carne, and we make every plate fresh to order. This is easy to do because the plates are very simple to assemble and the cheese melts when it meets with the hot chili. One plate is perfect for three people.*

3 cups Berghoff Chili con Carne (page 24)

1 (16-ounce) bag tortilla chips

1½ cups shredded Cheddar cheese

1½ cups prepared guacamole

¾ cup sour cream, plus extra for garnish

¾ cup prepared salsa

Chopped green onions, sliced, for garnish

Canned jalapeños, drained, for garnish

Heat the chili in a large pot until very hot, stirring from the bottom often to prevent burning. For each 10-inch plate, distribute 36 taco chips evenly. Top each with 1 cup of hot chili, ½ cup of cheese, ½ cup of guacamole, ¼ cup of sour cream, and ¼ cup of salsa. Garnish each plate as desired with a dollop of sour cream in the middle, some chopped green onions, and sliced jalapeños.

**VARIATION**

Substitute prepared canned chili of choice for Berghoff Chili con Carne. Heat until very hot, and follow the rest of the directions.

## ORIGINAL NACHOS

In 1943, a group of army wives from Fort Duncan, Eagle Pass, Texas, drove across the border to Piedras Negras, Mexico, to the Victory Club restaurant. The only staff member on duty was the maître d' Ignacio Anaya, nicknamed "Nachos." To accompany their drinks he improvised a snack: fried tortilla chips from the bar, topped with melted Cheddar cheese, garnished with sliced jalapeños. The army wives devoured them and dubbed them Nachos *especiales*.

# Berghoff Bar Nuts Four Ways

**Serves 8/Makes 1½ quarts**

*Nuts are the perfect snack to go with drinks, and they have been served at the Berghoff bar since 1898. Peanuts are crunchy and salty, but three of our Berghoff nuts are sweet. Cynics suggest that bars offer free nuts because the salt increases thirst, which increases drinking. But there is another reason: Peanuts are good food. They are high in protein, healthy (monosaturated) fat, B vitamins, and antioxidants, including resveratrol, a powerful antioxidant that is also found in red wine. We always encourage eating while drinking. For people with peanut allergies, just substitute salted cashews or salted, shelled pistachios in the following recipes.*

## SAVORY SPICY PEANUTS

2 pounds lightly salted cocktail peanuts

2 tablespoons olive oil

1 teaspoon garlic powder

1 teaspoon freshly ground black pepper

½ teaspoon ground red pepper

Preheat the oven to 350°F. Line two large baking sheets with parchment paper and spray with nonstick cooking spray.

In a medium-size bowl, toss the peanuts with the oil until combined. Sprinkle the remaining ingredients on top and mix well.

Divide the peanut mixture in half and spread evenly on the baking sheets. Bake the coated nuts until light golden brown, 16 to 18 minutes. Let cool to room temperature.

Store in an airtight container at room temperature for up to 2 weeks.

## CANDIED PEANUTS

**2 pounds lightly salted cocktail peanuts**

**⅓ cup honey**

**⅓ cup sugar**

## PEANUTS AT THE WORLD FAIR

In 1893, when Herman was selling his beer to fairgoers from a booth on the Midway outside Chicago's Columbian Exposition, he came across peanuts in a new and different form.

Another German immigrant, Frederick William Rueckheim, who left Hamburg in 1869 and came to Chicago in 1872, mass-produced his mixture of popcorn, molasses, and peanuts and introduced it at the fair. It was packed in the familiar red, white, and blue box with the Cracker Jack logo and the image of Sailor Jack (modeled after Rueckheim's young grandson Robert) and his dog, Bingo.

Preheat the oven to 350°F. Line two large baking sheets with parchment paper and spray with nonstick cooking spray.

In a medium-size bowl, toss the peanuts with the honey until combined. Sprinkle the sugar on top and mix well.

Divide the peanut mixture in half and spread evenly on the baking sheets. Bake until light golden brown, 16 to 18 minutes.

Let cool to room temperature. Break into small pieces. Store in an airtight container at room temperature for up to 2 weeks.

## VARIATIONS

Salted cashews or salted, shelled pistachios can be substituted for peanuts in the following recipes.

Sweet and Spicy Peanuts: To the Candied Peanuts recipe, add 1 teaspoon of freshly ground black pepper and ½ teaspoon of ground red pepper and prepare according to the directions.

Sweet Asian Peanuts: To Candied Peanuts recipe, add 2 tablespoons of sesame seeds and 2 tablespoons of sesame oil and prepare according to the directions.

# Berghoff Relish Tray

**Serves 8**

*Before we called them crudités, the relish tray was a fixture on turn-of-the-century dinner tables, including my grandmother Carlyn's. I still have her cut-glass relish dish. Our menu from 1914 has a "Relishes" section that lists French Olives, Genuine Dill Pickle, Genuine English Chow Chow, and Celery. By 1932, the relish section expanded with sliced tomatoes, cucumbers, radishes, green olives, ripe olives, asparagus vinaigrette, coleslaw, and green peppers. Customers loved crisp vegetables then and they love them today. My recipe has a lot of vegetables, because skimpy vegetables look pathetic on a platter. Vegetables are wholesome and healthy, so indulge! My twist on tradition is to serve these with a Green Onion Dip (page 11).*

16 spears blanched asparagus

16 trimmed, blanched green beans

16 (4-inch-long) celery ribs

16 (4-inch-long) carrot sticks

16 dill pickle spears

16 sweet baby pickles, gherkins, or cornichons

16 radishes, trimmed, halved

16 drained black olives

16 drained pimiento-stuffed green olives

Green onions, halved lengthwise, for garnish

To blanch asparagus and green beans: Place the vegetables in separate large shallow sieves with handles. Immerse each sieve in boiling, lightly salted water for 4 to 5 minutes. Remove the sieve and hold under cold running water until the vegetables are room temperature. Drain well.

Arrange the blanched vegetables and the other ingredients in clusters on a large, chilled platter. Cover and refrigerate until ready to serve. Garnish with green onions and serve with Green Onion Dip.

# Green Onion Dip

**Serves 8/Makes 2 cups**

*Dehydrated soup mixes first hit the American market in the 1940s. Lipton Onion Soup, introduced around 1952, became famous as a dip when, in 1954, a now-nameless California cook mixed an envelope of dehydrated Lipton Onion Soup with sour cream. Called California Dip, its fame spread across the country. By 1958, the recipe was printed on the Lipton Onion Soup mix box, and it is still popular today. My twist? Fresh green onion instead of dried onion, and a mixture of light sour cream and light mayonnaise.*

**1½ cups light sour cream**

**¾ cup finely chopped green onion (white and green parts)**

**⅓ cup light mayonnaise**

**1 tablespoon grated yellow onion**

**1 tablespoon lemon juice**

**1 teaspoon hot red pepper sauce**

**1 teaspoon finely grated lemon zest**

**1 teaspoon freshly ground black pepper**

**Kosher salt**

In a 1-quart bowl, mix all the ingredients well. Cover and refrigerate for at least 2 hours, or overnight. Serve as a dip with crudités.

## A BEER STONE?

Beer stein literally means "beer stone," and comes from the German *Steinkrug* (stone mug). Originally, beer mugs were made of stoneware or glass (a *Glaskrug*). Their generic name was *Maßkrug*, meaning "dosage-gauged jug," and held about one liter of beer. They still do. The word *Steinkrug* was shortened in English to *stein* and combined with *Bier* (beer). In Germany, lavishly decorated and colored stoneware biersteins are tourist novelties and rarely used for drinking. Exceptions are collectible steins with Bavarian motifs. The lid that you see on some *Steinkrugs*, however, is not just a novelty. During the late 1400s, in the summertime, central Europe was plagued by huge swarms of flies. Several German principalities passed laws requiring that food and beverage containers be covered, hence the hinged lid on the *Steinkrug*. It not only keeps out flies but keeps the beer from spilling when you are swinging your arms in time with a drinking song during Oktoberfest.

# Sausage Wellingtons

**Serves 8**

*Sausages wrapped in pastry are found in the United States, England, Australia, Germany, and Canada under different names: pigs in blankets, franks in jackets, biscuit dogs, fingers in a Band-Aid, wiener winks, kilted sausages, monkeys undercover, and—probably the origin of the Berghoff's bar snack—Wurstchen im Shlafrock, or "sausage in a nightgown." The sausage, of course, is what makes or breaks the snack. At the Berghoff bar we cook, then wrap up the authentic bratwurst in our house-made pastry, tucking in both ends, and bake it. It does indeed look like a sausage in a long old-fashioned neck-to-toe nightgown. At home, follow this recipe using two packages—which yields eight pieces—of convenient refrigerated ready-to-use pizza dough—or you can use roll and cut one recipe of our homemade pizza dough (page 119) to yield eight pieces.*

8 traditional, uncooked bratwurst

2 (12-ounce) bottles Berghoff beer, preferably dark

2 (11-ounce) tubes (10 inches long) refrigerated pizza dough

½ cup Dusseldorf or coarse-grained brown mustard, plus extra for dipping

1 egg beaten with 1 tablespoon water

Preheat the oven to 400°F. Oil or spray with cooking spray two baking sheets.

Cook the bratwurst: Prick the sausages with a fork in several places. Place them in a single layer in a large saucepan or skillet and cover with the beer. Bring to a boil. Decrease the heat immediately, and simmer until the sausages are cooked through, about 15 minutes. Drain well. Let cool to room temperature.

Prepare the Sausage Wellingtons: On a clean, dry, lightly floured surface, spread out the prepared pizza dough flat. It should measure approximately 12 by 17 inches. Cut in half vertically and again horizontally, creating four rectangles long enough to cover the sausage ends and wide enough to roll up the sausage and seal around it.

Spread 1 tablespoon of mustard on each dough rectangle. Brush the edges of the dough lightly with water. Lay a sausage link in the middle and roll the dough tightly around the sausage, making sure to maintain the shape of the sausage. Seal the seam of each by pinching well. Bring the ends of the dough around the ends of the sausage and pinch well to seal. Cut off any excess dough and discard. Place the rolls, seam side down, on the prepared pans. Repeat with the remaining sheets of dough and sausages. Brush the tops with beaten egg.

Bake in the preheated oven until golden brown, 18 to 20 minutes.

Serve hot, sliced diagonally in segments as a bar snack or cut in half as a sandwich for lunch. Serve with plenty of brown mustard for dipping.

*Note:* These may be prepared and frozen for up to 2 weeks until ready to bake. Freeze flat on a parchment paper–lined tray. When frozen, transfer to resealable plastic bags, date, and label. These may also be served as an entrée.

### VARIATIONS

Use 1 tablespoon of sautéed diced mushrooms or sautéed sliced onions, or drained sauerkraut to garnish the sausages before wrapping and baking.

Instead of prepared refrigerated pizza dough, prepare one recipe of plain or caraway pizza dough (page 119). Divide the dough recipe in half. Roll out each half on a lightly floured surface into a 12 by 17-inch rectangle. Proceed with the recipe.

Instead of bratwurst, use traditional Thuringer and cook according to the directions on the package. You may substitute any fresh smoked or unsmoked sausage you like, and cook it in beer. But it is best to use a sausage that is about 6 inches long.

# Stuffed Celery Three Ways

**Serves 8/Makes 32 stuffed celery ribs (2 cups of filling)**

*Crisp fresh celery ribs stuffed with pimiento cream cheese appeared on my grandmother Carlyn's dinner table every Sunday. This old-fashioned treat tastes every bit as good to me and to my kids today. We serve it as a snack at the Berghoff bar, but I also have developed some tasty variations.*

*Instead of stuffing these fillings into celery, use as a spread or filling for panini. Use to stuff deviled eggs. and use as a dip for vegetables.*

### PIMIENTO CHEESE–STUFFED CELERY

1 cup light mayonnaise

1 (4-ounce) jar diced pimiento, well drained

½ to 1 teaspoon Worcestershire sauce

1 teaspoon finely grated yellow onion

¼ teaspoon kosher salt

⅛ teaspoon cayenne

1¼ cups finely shredded sharp Cheddar cheese

32 (4-inch-long) celery ribs

Paprika, for garnish

In a medium-size bowl, combine the mayonnaise, pimiento, Worcestershire, onion, salt, and cayenne. Mix well. Fold in the Cheddar. Cover and refrigerate for at least 2 hours before using.

Spread 1 tablespoon of filling inside each celery rib, smoothing the top. (Or pipe from a pastry bag fitted with a ¼-inch plain tip.) Cover and chill until ready to serve.

Sprinkle the tops lightly with paprika before serving.

### VARIATION

For more pronounced pimiento flavor and color, use a 7-ounce jar of pimientos, well drained.

*Note:* To make a disposable pastry bag, fill a 1-gallon resealable plastic bag with the filling mixture. Using a sharp scissors, cut off ¼ inch of one corner on the diagonal. Squeeze out the filling by twisting the bag from the top.

## SMOKED GOUDA AND DRIED TOMATO–STUFFED CELERY

⅔ cup light mayonnaise

2 tablespoons buttermilk

1 teaspoon finely grated yellow onion

½ teaspoon paprika

1½ cups lightly packed, grated, smoked Gouda cheese

⅓ cup finely chopped drained oil-packed dried tomatoes

Kosher salt and freshly ground black pepper

32 (4-inch-long) celery ribs

In a medium-size bowl, combine the mayonnaise, buttermilk, onion, and paprika. Whisk to mix. Fold in the cheese and tomatoes and mix well. Season to taste with salt and pepper. Cover and refrigerate for at least 2 hours before stuffing the celery according to the Pimiento Cheese–Stuffed Celery recipe.

## CRAB-STUFFED CELERY

1 (8-ounce) package cream cheese, softened

1 (6-ounce) can crabmeat, well drained

¼ cup sour cream

1 tablespoon grated onion

1½ tablespoons lemon juice

1½ teaspoons dried dill, or 3 tablespoons fresh, minced

Kosher salt and freshly ground black pepper

32 (4-inch-long) celery ribs

Paprika, for garnish

In a medium-size bowl, combine all the ingredients, except the celery and paprika, and stir gently to mix well. Cover and refrigerate for at least 2 hours before stuffing the celery according to the Pimiento Cheese–Stuffed Celery recipe. Sprinkle the stuffed celery with paprika and serve.

### VARIATION

To make a crab patty melt: Spread the filling over toasted English muffin halves, top each with one slice of Cheddar cheese, and heat in the oven or under the broiler until the filling is hot and the cheese melts.

# Fresh Baked Pretzels

**Makes 12 medium-size or 24 small pretzels**

*Pretzels are one of the world's oldest snacks. Great-grandfather Herman ate them in Germany as a boy and here in America as an adult. It was natural that they would find their way into the Berghoff bar. Traditionally, shaped pretzel dough is briefly boiled in water, just like bagels, before being baked. This brief boiling gives both pretzels and bagels shiny crusts and a very chewy texture. I omitted the step of boiling the shaped dough when I developed our pretzel recipe for the home kitchen, so this pretzel is easy to shape and bake. It has a nice soft crust, easy to bite, easy to chew. It is best baked and eaten on the same day. Pretzels are fun for kids and grown-ups alike to shape. We recommend eating these pretzels with any Berghoff beer or a frosty mug of Berghoff Root Beer.*

4½ cups unbleached all-purpose flour, plus additional for kneading

1 (¼-ounce) package (2¼ teaspoons) instant yeast

2 tablespoons sugar

2 teaspoons kosher salt

1½ cups warm water

4 tablespoons (½ stick) unsalted butter, melted

1 large egg yolk, lightly beaten

1 large egg white, well beaten with 1 tablespoon water

Pretzel (coarse) salt, as needed

Preheat the oven to 450°F. Do not use a convection oven for this recipe.

To mix in a mixer: In the bowl of a standing mixer fitted with the paddle attachment, combine the flour, yeast, sugar, and salt, and stir to mix; add the water, butter, and egg yolk, and mix on low until the dough pulls away from the side of the bowl.

Fit the mixer with the dough hook and knead the dough at the lowest speed until the dough is smooth and elastic, about 8 minutes, adding some or all of the remaining flour as needed. Cover with plastic wrap lightly sprayed with cooking spray and let rise in a warm place until doubled, about 1 hour.

To mix by hand: In a 4-quart bowl, combine the flour, yeast, sugar, and salt, and whisk to mix; add the water, butter, and egg yolk and, using a large spoon, stir until the dough pulls away from the side of the bowl.

Remove the spoon and, using your hands, knead the dough right in the bowl until the dough is smooth and elastic, about 8 minutes, adding some or all of the remaining flour as needed. Cover with plastic wrap lightly sprayed with cooking spray and let rise in a warm place until doubled, about 1 hour.

To mix in a food processor: In the work bowl of a large-capacity (14-cup) food processor fitted with the plastic dough blade, combine the flour, yeast, sugar, and salt, and pulse to mix. Add the water, butter, and egg yolk, and pulse until the dough pulls away from the side of the bowl and forms a cohesive mass. Add additional flour as needed through the feed tube.

To shape the pretzels: Turn out the dough on a lightly floured board and knead briefly, about 1 minute. Cut the dough into twelve equal-size pieces. Roll out each dough piece into a 24-inch-long rope. Make a U shape with the rope. Holding the ends of the rope, cross them over each other and press the ends down onto the bottom

## PRETZEL PEDIGREE

According to some historians, the pretzel is the world's oldest snack food.

It was invented by a now-nameless Italian monk-baker in AD 610, who rewarded his students by baking scraps of dough in the shape of the way they prayed—with arms folded across the chest. He called them *pretiolas*, Latin for "little rewards." *Pretiolas* spread throughout Europe and became symbols of good luck, long life, and prosperity. German children wore pretzels tied on strings around their necks at New Year's and pretzels crowned the tops of Christmas trees.

In 1510, Turkish soldiers tried to invade Vienna, Austria, by digging tunnels underneath the city. The pretzel bakers, working at night, heard them, alarmed the city, and helped fight off the invaders. The grateful Austrian emperor commissioned a special coat of arms for them, still used today: a charging lion and a pretzel.

Until the 1600s, pretzels were soft. The hard pretzel is credited to a nameless seventeenth-century baker who fell asleep and overbaked the soft pretzels.

According to historians, pretzels (and their recipes) came to America on shipboard with the first colonists and were traded with Native Americans.

In 1861, Julius Sturgis opened the first commercial pretzel bakery in America in Lititz, Pennsylvania.

of the U to seal, forming a "pretzel shape." For small pretzels, cut the dough into 24 equal-size pieces. Roll out each dough piece into a 12-inch-long rope and shape as directed.

Gently place each pretzel on a parchment paper–lined baking sheet (two pans). Brush the tops lightly with the egg white mixture. Sprinkle each with ½ teaspoon of coarse salt, or to taste. Bake in the preheated oven for 14 to 16 minutes, or until browned and firm. Transfer to a cooling rack and let cool for 5 to 10 minutes before serving.

### VARIATIONS

Cheese Pretzels: Add 2 cups of grated white Cheddar cheese (8 ounces) with the dry ingredients and proceed with the recipe. Or add 1 cup of grated Parmesan cheese (4 ounces) to the flour and proceed with the recipe, then sprinkle a second cup of grated Parmesan (4 ounces) on the egg white–brushed pretzels before baking.

Caraway Pretzels: Add 4 teaspoons of caraway seeds to the flour and proceed with the recipe.

Top with ½ cup of coarse salt before baking.

Bacon Pretzels: Add ½ cup of bacon bits (from a jar or package) to the flour and proceed with the recipe. Sprinkle with kosher salt as needed and ¼ cup of bacon bits before baking.

Chocolate Chip Pretzels: Increase the butter to ½ cup and the sugar to ⅓ cup, and prepare the dough according to the recipe. Add to the finished dough 1 cup of chocolate chips, kneading only long enough to incorporate the chips. Dust the baked pretzels with 1½ cups of confectioners' sugar.

Cinnamon-Raisin Pretzels: Increase the butter to ½ cup and the sugar to ½ cup, and add 2 teaspoons of ground cinnamon. Prepare the dough according to the recipe. Add to the finished dough ½ cup of dark raisins cut in half, kneading only long enough to incorporate. Dust the baked pretzels well with 1½ cups of confectioners' sugar.

Mini-Pretzels: Make half-size versions of any of the above by dividing the dough into 24 equal-size pieces and rolling into 12-inch-long ropes. Then proceed with the rest of the recipe as directed.

Café Manhattan Clam Chowder

# CHAPTER 2

## SOUPS

# Big Bowls

Soups have been part of the Berghoff Café since the first menus were printed, and they're among my earliest food memories. My namesake, grandmother Carlyn, was a great cook, and her soups were meals in themselves because they all had big hunks of meats, vegetables, and croutons.

The croutons were made from day-old bread that she diced and fried in fresh butter until crispy. Her soups were fine with me when she was serving chicken noodle soup or her potato soup with chunks of onion and potatoes. But when it came to her split pea soup, I hated that it was green and that it came with big pink lumps of ham that lay in ambush for me at the bottom of the bowl. I have since learned to like split pea soup.

My own kids love my tomato soup and vegetable-noodle soup, which I customize for their liking by dividing the broth into batches, then adding vegetables. Lindsey likes only carrots, celery, peppers, and onion; Sarah and Todd will eat everything but cauliflower and mushrooms. Sarah is

the only one who likes lentils, so I freeze it in small containers to have it handy for her. I am a great believer in making double batches and freezing soup in meal-size containers.

The 1914 Berghoff menu listed two surprisingly contemporary soups at two old-fashioned prices: Chili con Carne and Clam Chowder, both at twenty-five cents per bowl. How they came to be on this early menu was not too surprising. Chile con Carne was sold at a State of Texas stand at the World's Fair in 1893, when Herman was selling his Berghoff beer from a saloon tent on the Midway. And when he had first come to New York two decades earlier, clam chowder with tomatoes (later known as Manhattan clam chowder) had already been known there since the mid-1800s.

Today at the Berghoff Café, we are surrounded by extra vegetables and meats in the sixteen refrigerators that we share with the restaurant, bar, and catering services, so chef Matt Reichel is never short of ingredients to reuse and recycle. Although he tries to keep them seasonal, as he reinvents versions of gazpacho in summer and potato soup in winter, there are two soups that customers want all year long: Alsatian Onion Soup and our Homemade Chicken Spaetzle Soup. In addition to such regular features, Matt makes daily specials, too.

The soups in this chapter are all hearty, simple, and satisfying, and they can all either begin the meal or be the meal if you serve them with bread and salad. Except for Beer-Cheese Soup, all the soups can be doubled and frozen.

# Homemade Chicken Broth and Chicken Meat

**Makes approximately 2 quarts broth, 2 pounds meat**

*I like the flavor of homemade chicken broth. Homemade broth has no preservatives or chemicals added, it is not overly salty, and you get two for the price of one: broth and chicken meat for the price of a chicken.*

1 (3-pound) frying chicken

3 carrots, peeled and halved

3 celery ribs, halved

1 medium-size yellow onion, peeled and halved

3 sprigs fresh thyme, or 1 teaspoon dried

2 peeled garlic cloves

1 bay leaf

3 quarts cold water

1 teaspoon kosher salt

Place all the ingredients in an 8- to 10-quart stockpot. Bring to a boil over high heat. Decrease the heat immediately, cover, and let simmer for 1 hour.

Remove the pot from the heat. Strain the broth through a colander, reserving the chicken. Let the broth cool to room temperature, then refrigerate, covered, overnight. When ready to use, skim off and discard any surface fat.

Let the chicken cool to room temperature. Remove the chicken meat from the bones, and discard the bones and skin. With a fork, shred the meat (or wearing disposable plastic gloves, use your fingers to do this). Refrigerate until ready to use.

# Chili con Carne

**Serves 8 to 10**

*Chili con Carne has been on the café's menu since our first surviving printed menu of 1914, and possibly even before. Chili con carne was featured and sold at the 1893 Columbian Exposition in Chicago, where Great-grandfather Herman must surely have had a bowlful. The café's contemporary version is a year-round favorite and we also use it in the nachos that we serve at the bar. We like the texture of coarsely ground beef, and you can ask the butcher to coarsely grind it for you. The chili powder we use is the mixed seasoning, not straight ground hot chiles.*

3 tablespoons vegetable oil

3 cups chopped yellow onion

3 pounds coarsely ground beef chuck

2 tablespoons minced fresh garlic

1 (12-ounce) bottle Berghoff Original Lager

2 tablespoons chili seasoning mix

1 (6-ounce) can tomato paste

2 teaspoons fresh lemon juice

1 teaspoon hot red pepper sauce

1 (28-ounce) can kidney beans, drained and rinsed

1 (28-ounce) can chopped tomatoes and their juice

1 seeded, chopped fresh jalapeño

Kosher salt and freshly ground black pepper

Oyster crackers, for serving

Chopped onions, for serving

Sliced canned jalapeños, for serving

Grated Cheddar cheese, for serving

Heat the oil in an 8- to 10-quart stockpot over medium heat. Add the onion and cook, stirring, until translucent but not brown. Add the beef and cook, stirring and breaking into small pieces, until the meat browns. Add the garlic and cook, stirring, for 2 minutes.

Add the beer, chili seasoning, and tomato paste and cook, stirring, for 10 minutes. Add the lemon juice, hot pepper sauce, kidney beans, tomatoes, and jalapeño and heat through. When the chili comes to a simmer, cook for 10 minutes. Season to taste with salt and pepper.

Serve in individual bowls, and add your favorite topping.

Substitute ground pork or turkey—or a combination of ground meats—for the beef.

To increase the spiciness, increase the hot red pepper sauce to taste, or offer bottled hot sauce so everyone can add it to individual servings as desired.

# CHILI CON CARNE: NOT MEXICAN!

Chili con carne did not originate in Mexico but in the American Southwest, and legends still surround it. Chili's invention is credited to Texas cowboys and adventurers traveling to California gold fields who needed nourishing food, such as stew, that could be cooked en route.

Another story says it was the Texas Lavanderas, or "washerwomen" who followed nineteenth-century Texas armies, who first made a stew of chile peppers plus goat or venison.

Inmates of Texas prisons in the mid- to late 1800s also laid claim to chile con carne, which used the cheapest possible cuts of beef.

In the 1880s when San Antonio was a wild, open town, Latino women called "chili queens" sold a stew called chili from open-air stalls in the town marketplace.

Not only the stew but its seasoning has rival claims. Fort Worth Texas chili lovers credit DeWitt Clinton Pendery with selling his own dried seasoning blend of chiles to cafés and residents under the name of Mexican Chili Supply Company. His products are still sold today by family members.

But San Antonio chili buffs swear that chili powder was the invention of a German immigrant in New Braunfels, Texas, named William Gebhardt. He trademarked his Eagle Brand Chili Powder in 1896 and it is still sold today.

This much is history: In 1893, the State of Texas set up a San Antonio Chili Stand at the Columbian Exposition in Chicago. And we know that Herman Berghoff was also at the fair, selling his beer from a tent on the Midway.

# Alsatian Onion Soup

**Serves 8 to 10**

*We always have onions and apples on hand at the restaurant, as well as chicken, beef, and vegetable broth. So this is my twist on traditional French onion soup. I add apples, a dash of sherry, and a big crouton topped with Muenster cheese, which is baked until golden and bubbly. It is one of our customers' favorite soups, and one of mine, too. If you use vegetable broth, it becomes a vegetarian soup. You can prepare it days in advance, refrigerate and reheat it, and add the crouton when you are ready to serve. The most important step is browning the onions well: the time this takes will depend on your stove.*

2 tablespoons vegetable oil

5 cups (about 1½ pounds) yellow onion, halved vertically, sliced ⅛ inch thick

2 quarts beef, chicken, or vegetable broth

2 bay leaves

⅛ teaspoon red pepper flakes

2 cups peeled, julienned Granny Smith apples

3 tablespoons dry sherry

Kosher salt and freshly ground black pepper

8 ½-inch-thick slices of baguette, toasted

8 slices Muenster cheese

Heat the oil in an 8- to 10-quart stockpot over medium heat. Add the onion and cook, stirring often, until golden brown (but not burned), 15 to 25 minutes. Add the broth, bay leaves, and red pepper flakes and bring to a boil. Decrease the heat and simmer for 30 minutes. Discard the bay leaves.

Stir in the apples and sherry and let simmer until the apples are just tender, 10 minutes. Season to taste with salt and pepper.

Garnish each bowl with a crouton topped with a slice of Muenster cheese. Place under the broiler until the cheese melts.

The soup may be made (without croutons) up to four days ahead and refrigerated, covered. Reheat in a microwave or on the range top. Then garnish with the cheese-topped crouton and broil according to the recipe directions.

# Café Manhattan Clam Chowder

**Serves 8 to 10**

*New England–style clam chowder has milk and/or cream. Manhattan clam chowder is broth based, has no milk or cream, and traditionally has tomatoes added. Our chef Matt Reichel puts his own twist on tradition by using bell peppers instead of tomatoes, making for a very special chowder.*

3 slices uncooked bacon, diced

1 cup chopped yellow onion

½ cup diced celery

½ tablespoon minced fresh garlic

3 (6½-ounce) cans minced clams

2 (8-ounce} bottles clam juice

1 to 2 teaspoons dried thyme

1 to 2 bay leaves

2 cups peeled and diced russet potatoes (2 large)

½ cup seeded and diced red bell pepper

½ cup seeded and diced yellow bell pepper

½ cup seeded and diced green bell pepper

Kosher salt and freshly ground black pepper

3 tablespoons chopped fresh flat-leaf parsley, for garnish

Oyster crackers, for serving

Sauté the bacon in an 8- to 10-quart stockpot over medium heat, stirring, until crisp and golden brown. Using a slotted spoon, remove the bacon, drain on paper towels, and set aside. Pour off the bacon fat into a heatproof container. Return 1 tablespoon of bacon fat to the pot.

Add the onion and celery to the pot and sauté, stirring, until tender, about 5 minutes. Add the garlic and sauté, stirring, for 2 minutes.

Strain the canned clams, reserving the juice separately. Add the bottled and reserved clam juice to the stockpot. Bring to a simmer. Add the thyme, bay leaves, and potatoes. Cook until the potatoes are tender, about 25 minutes.

Add the clams and peppers. Bring to a simmer and cook for 10 minutes. Remove and discard the bay leaves. Season to taste with salt and pepper. Garnish individual bowls with chopped parsley, and serve with oyster crackers.

# Homemade Chicken Spaetzle Soup

**Serves 8 to 10**

*This is the Berghoff version of chicken noodle soup, with spaetzle instead of noodles. I make it with homemade chicken stock and use the meat from the chicken stock in the soup. But you can also use prepared chicken broth and leftover cooked chicken. I like to use a mixture of chicken breast and thigh meat, but you can use either according to your preference. The soup can be made, except for the spaetzle, in advance. Refrigerate it, then reheat it when ready to serve, and add the spaetzle.*

2 cups Spaetzle (page 85)

2 tablespoons vegetable oil

1½ cups finely chopped carrots

1 cup finely chopped onion

1 cup finely chopped celery

2 bay leaves

Pinch of freshly ground black pepper

2 quarts prepared or homemade chicken broth (page 23)

1 cup thinly sliced leeks, white and pale green parts only

3 cups boneless, skinless shredded or diced cooked chicken

Kosher salt and freshly ground black pepper

If the spaetzle have been refrigerated, let them come to room temperature while you prepare the soup.

Heat the oil in an 8- to 10-quart stockpot over medium heat. Add the carrots, onion, celery, bay leaves, and a pinch of pepper and sauté, stirring occasionally, until the vegetables are tender, 5 to 8 minutes. Add the chicken broth, leeks, and diced chicken, and bring to a simmer. Season to taste with salt and pepper. Let simmer slowly for 30 minutes. Remove and discard the bay leaves.

To serve, place 2 rounded tablespoons of spaetzle in the bottom of each soup bowl. Ladle in the hot chicken soup.

**VARIATION**

Substitute your favorite cooked egg noodles for the spaetzle.

# Beer-Cheese Soup

**Makes eight 1-cup servings**

*Beer-cheese soup is traditionally very German but also popular in the Midwest, where fall and winter weather makes it a welcome bowl of warmth. You can use any Berghoff beer with this, but my favorite is Berghoff Original Amber. The only tricks to making this recipe are using freshly grated cheese (packaged pregrated cheese from the supermarket doesn't melt well) and not letting the soup boil during or after adding the cheese. I like to serve it with a plain or caraway pretzel (page 19), or with freshly popped popcorn. Put the bowl of popcorn on the table and let everyone add it to the soup as they eat.*

4 tablespoons (½ stick) unsalted butter

1½ cups finely chopped leeks, white and pale green parts only (about 2 medium-size) (see Note)

2 teaspoons finely chopped garlic

1 bay leaf

½ cup all-purpose flour

3 cups whole milk, at room temperature

2 cups chicken broth

1 (12-ounce) bottle Berghoff amber beer

1 tablespoon Worcestershire sauce

1 teaspoon mustard powder

¼ teaspoon kosher salt

¼ teaspoon freshly ground black pepper

2 cups freshly shredded mild Cheddar cheese

2 cups freshly shredded Swiss cheese

Fresh Baked Pretzels (page 17) or freshly popped popcorn, for serving

Heat the butter in an 8- to 10-quart stockpot over medium heat. Add the leeks, garlic, and bay leaf, and cook, stirring occasionally, until the leeks are tender, about 6 minutes. Decrease the heat to medium-low, sprinkle the flour over the leek mixture, and cook for 3 minutes, stirring often. Slowly whisk in the milk, 1 cup at a time, and cook, whisking, until smooth and fully thickened. (This takes some time, so don't try to rush this step.) Slowly add the broth and beer, whisking constantly until fully incorporated. Bring to a simmer and cook for 5 minutes, whisking occasionally from the bottom to prevent sticking and burning. Remove and discard the bay leaf. Stir in the Worcestershire, mustard, salt, and pepper.

Add the cheese by handfuls, stirring constantly. Cook over medium heat without boiling until the cheese is melted, 3 to 4 minutes. Keep warm until ready to serve. Stir well before serving with fresh pretzels or a big bowl of fresh popcorn.

The soup may be made ahead and refrigerated for up to 4 days. Reheat in the microwave on medium power or on the stovetop, in a hot-water bath, until hot.

## VARIATIONS

Instead of grating cheese at home, have the deli slice the cheese thinly. Then add to the soup slice by slice.

Use half sharp and half mild Cheddar.

Substitute vegetable broth for the chicken broth.

*Note:* Leeks are available in the produce section already cleaned and ready to use. If you buy whole leeks, cut off the root end and discard. Then cut off the upper dark green parts and save for soup stock. Use only the white and pale green parts of the leeks. Cut the leeks horizontally into 2-inch lengths. Separate the ribs and soak and swish in a bowl of cold water or rinse under cold running water to remove the sand or grit.

# Flavor Boosters for Soups

Sometimes a soup tastes a little flat, as if something is missing. When that happens, try one from this list of simple flavor boosters. What you reach for depends on whether the soup is broth or cream based. Try to match the soup's main ingredients to the add-ins.

## For broth-based soups

- 1 tablespoon prepared pesto (vegetable and chicken-noodle/rice soups)
- 1 tablespoon tomato paste or tomato purée from a tube (vegetable, chicken, turkey, and tomato soups)
- ½ to 1 teaspoon prepared garlic purée (almost any soup)
- 1 teaspoon mild or hot curry powder (sweet potato, squash, carrot, and corn soups)
- 1 tablespoon dried minced onion (almost any soup)
- 1 chicken, beef, or vegetable bouillon cube (almost any soup)
- 1 teaspoon freshly ground black or white pepper (any soup)
- 1 teaspoon caraway seeds (cabbage, cauliflower, and potato soup)
- 2 tablespoons grated Parmesan (vegetable, chicken, turkey, tomato, potato, onion, and mushroom soups)
- Cooked white rice, as needed (adds body to almost any brothy soup)
- ½ cup dry white wine (almost any soup; let simmer for at least 5 minutes)

## For cream-based or thick, puréed soups

- ½ to 1 teaspoon prepared garlic purée (any soup)
- 1 tablespoon dried minced onion (any soup)
- 1 chicken, beef, or vegetable bouillon cube (any soup)
- 1 teaspoon freshly ground black or white pepper (any soup)
- Canned coconut milk to taste (sweet potato, squash, corn, and carrot soups)
- Heavy cream or half-and-half as needed (to reheat, enrich, and thicken)
- A dollop of sour cream or crème fraîche (split pea, sweet potato, squash, carrot, and tomato soups)
- A drizzle of puréed jarred sweet red peppers (potato, squash, carrot, sweet potato, and corn soups)
- 1 or more tablespoons dehydrated mashed potatoes (to thicken and enrich almost any cream or puréed soup)
- ⅛ to ¼ teaspoon ground cinnamon (squash, carrot, and sweet potato soups)

# Potato Soup

**Serves 8 to 10**

*Potato soup is as simple and as satisfying as it gets. This is my favorite version. It has all the flavor of grand-mother Carlyn's potato soup but without the big pieces of potatoes and onions that sometime required cutting with a fork to eat. I serve this potato soup for family, friends, and company. I make it without bacon and with organic vegetable broth for my vegetarian friends and for my daughter Sarah.*

2 slices uncooked bacon, diced

3 tablespoons unsalted butter

1 cup diced yellow onion

1 cup diced leeks, white and
pale green parts only

¼ cup all-purpose flour

1 bay leaf

1½ quarts chicken or vegetable
broth, preferably organic

3 cups diced, peeled russet potatoes

½ cup heavy cream or half-and-half

1 teaspoon kosher salt

1 teaspoon ground white pepper

3 tablespoons minced fresh
parsley, for garnish

Cook the bacon in an 8- to 10-quart stockpot over medium heat, stirring, until golden brown. Using a slotted spoon, remove the bacon, drain on a paper towel, and set aside. Discard the bacon fat. Return the pot to the heat and melt the butter. Add the onion and leeks, and cook, stirring, until the vegetables are tender but not browned, 3 to 5 minutes. Whisk in the flour and cook for 1 minute, stirring often. Slowly add the bay leaf and chicken broth, whisking constantly. Cook until thickened. Add the potatoes and cooked bacon, and bring to a simmer. Simmer until the potatoes are tender, 25 to 30 minutes, stirring often from the bottom to prevent the soup from sticking and burning.

Add the cream and let simmer for 5 minutes. Remove the pan from the heat. Remove and discard the bay leaf. Season to taste with salt and pepper. Serve in individual bowls garnished with parsley.

## VARIATIONS

For a vegetarian soup, omit the bacon and use vegetable broth.

Substitute sweet onions, such as Vidalia, in season.

Substitute Yukon Gold potatoes for the russets.

Substitute minced fresh chives or thyme for the parsley.

# Turkey, Okra, and Rice Soup

**Serve 8 to 10**

*This is one of the most popular soups year round at the Berghoff Café, maybe because the New Orleans flavor is exciting to Midwesterners. But it's popular with our chef Matt Reichel because he always has extra turkey breasts that he roasts for our Turkey Reuben sandwich (page 52). This is also a nice way to use up leftover holiday turkey. There are many blends of Creole seasoning mixes on the market; however, some may be more Cajun than Creole, and contain more cayenne. Also some have salt added. My advice is to carefully take a small taste before you add it to the soup, to ensure that you have the right amount of heat for your palate.*

2 tablespoons vegetable oil

1 cup finely chopped onion

1 cup finely chopped celery

1 cup finely chopped carrots

1 cup finely chopped leeks, white
and pale green parts only

2 bay leaves

⅛ teaspoon freshly ground black pepper

2 quarts chicken broth

3 cups diced boneless cooked turkey

¼ cup prepared Creole seasoning

1 (8-ounce) can chopped tomatoes with juice

Kosher salt

2 cups frozen cut okra, thawed

1 cup seeded and finely diced
green bell pepper

2 cups cooked white rice, for
serving (see Note)

Heat the oil in an 8- to 10-quart stockpot over medium heat. Add the onions, celery, carrots, leeks, bay leaves, and pepper. Sauté, stirring, until the vegetables are tender but not browned, 5 to 8 minutes. Add the chicken broth, turkey, Creole seasoning, and tomatoes, and let simmer slowly for 35 minutes. Adjust the seasoning to taste with salt.

Stir in the okra and simmer until just cooked, about 5 minutes. Add the diced green peppers and cook for 5 minutes. Serve the soup in individual bowls with 1 to 2 tablespoons of cooked rice in each.

## VARIATIONS

When fresh okra is available (May through October), substitute fresh for frozen.

Substitute cooked chicken for the turkey.

*Note:* To cook white rice: In a small saucepan, combine 1 cup of long-grain white rice with 1¾ cups of water, 1 teaspoon of kosher salt, and 1 teaspoon butter or olive oil. Bring to a boil, cover, decrease the heat, and simmer slowly until the water is completely absorbed, about 15 minutes. Remove the pan from the heat. Let rest, covered, for 5 minutes. Fluff with a fork and serve.

# DAY-AFTER-THANKSGIVING SOUP

Here is the Berghoff family traditional turkey soup that anyone can make because it's based on the leftover turkey bones and scraps, has three simple steps, and it can be customized with everybody's favorite vegetables and/or grains. First, put all the turkey bones and any scraps of meat or skin and any leftover vegetables (that don't have a sauce or are not potatoes) in a big stockpot, 12 to 20 gallons. Mine holds 20 gallons. (It helps to break the turkey carcass in half.) Next, cover with fresh cold tap water by 3 inches. Add 1 teaspoon each of dried thyme and sage, chopped garlic, and, if you like, 1 to 2 cups of white wine. Bring to a boil, Decrease the heat and simmer for 2 hours. Strain the broth through a big colander and save; discard everything else. Refrigerate overnight in covered containers. The next day, remove from the refrigerator and skim off and discard the surface fat. At this point you can freeze it in 2-quart containers, or start making the soup. Add your favorite chopped vegetables (white and sweet potatoes included), about 2 cups for every quart of broth, and ¼ cup of your favorite grain: uncooked rice, pearl barley (the Berghoff favorite), or even noodles. Season to taste with salt and pepper and cook until the vegetables and grain are tender.

Pimiento Cheese Panini

# CHAPTER 3

# SANDWICHES

# Something of Substance

Sandwiches were the very foundation of the café menu. Great-grandfather Herman's three sandwiches—corned beef, boiled ham, and a real frankfurter in natural casing—are still on the menu more than a century later. Sandwiches are wildly popular at the café today. I have updated the garnishes and

spreads, and also the breads. Back in Herman's day, customers could choose between rye bread, rye bread, and rye bread. There are many styles of rye bread, in addition to the version with caraway seeds in *The Berghoff Family Cookbook*. In this chapter I offer you a simple recipe for Berghoff Sandwich Rye with three flavor Variations: dill seeds, sauerkraut, or bacon and onion.

Today's panini are yesterday's grilled cheese sandwiches. Cheese sandwiches were always popular on the Berghoff Café menus, and my twist on tradition is to transform them into panini. In 1914, cheese sandwiches included pimiento, Swiss, and, stylishly listed "Fromage de Brie." In addition to these panini, I hope you will enjoy setting up a panini bar. It's great fun. (See The "Patini" Bar, page 41.) Panini are versatile for many occasions: to cook with your kids, for brunch or lunch, or for a family supper when you're too tired or too hot to cook a three-course dinner.

Growing up in the Berghoff family meant big Sunday dinners, and Sunday dinners always meant roasts. Roasts meant leftovers, and leftovers meant sandwiches. The sandwiches from my childhood were not garnished: just good cold meat sliced and piled high between two pieces of bread. Sometimes there was mayo, sometimes mustard, but many times just bread. I call them "naked sandwiches" because they have nothing to hide. And in the café today, we serve many of our most popular sandwiches—turkey, roast beef, corned beef—naked with condiments and pickle on the side. My kids go one step beyond naked and beyond open-face. Often they just roll up slices of meat or cheese and dip them in individual dishes of mustard or mayonnaise.

The café has a great hamburger, and what I believe is a great twist on the traditional Reuben, the Turkey Reuben, which is popular spring, summer, fall, and winter. The All-Day, All-Night Egg Sandwich dates back to the 1914 menu, and if you follow our recipe for the Real Thing Frankfurter, you'll see why it's a favorite with our café customers. Chef Matt Reichel created the Berghoff Sub, and we share his recipe for this enormously good sandwich, too.

## CHIPS WITH A TWIST

In 1853, George Crum, a chef at Moon's Lake House resort in Saratoga Springs, New York, had an entrée returned to the kitchen because the guest said Crum's french fries were too thick. Crum was so annoyed that he sliced potatoes paper thin, fried them crisp, and sent these back to the table. Not only that guest but also others loved Crum's potato chips, and they became a menu item, known for many years as Saratoga Chips. In 1895, a Cleveland, Ohio, entrepreneur named William Tappendon turned his barn into the first potato chip factory and started selling potato chips to grocery stores. By 1900, potato chip factories were producing America's favorite snack. When I was seven years old, my best friend, Linda, and I spent summers together in Michigan at the beach. My mom would bring us sandwiches and chips on paper plates. The wind would blow the chips away and the greedy birds would eat them—until that wonderful day when I thought of sticking the chips inside the sandwich. To this day, my kids and I eat our chips on the inside instead of on the side. This works for any sandwich with a soft filling or a spread such as butter or mayo that helps the chips stick. It's delicious and nutritious because we eat fewer chips.

# Pimiento Cheese Panini

**Serves 8**

*This is my twist on the traditional pimiento cheese sandwich that has been on the café menu since at least 1914. However, until I married my husband Jim—who was born and raised in the South—and met his marvelous mother, Mary Carol, I had forgotten all about it. Pimiento cheese is very Southern and it was Mary Carol who reintroduced me to one of my own family's favorites. For this panini recipe, I mix a double recipe of pimiento cheese, spread it on some interesting bread, tuck in some crisp cooked bacon and paper-thin ripe tomato slices, and pop it on a panini grill. You can also make the panini in a sauté pan. I like to serve this with a bowl of tomato soup.*

4 cups Pimiento Cheese (page 14)

1 pound sliced applewood-smoked bacon cooked, drained of excess fat

16 slices Berghoff Sandwich Rye (page 46), or good white sandwich bread

32 paper-thin slices ripe tomato

Melted butter, as needed, or olive oil nonstick cooking spray

Spread ½ cup of pimiento cheese on eight slices of bread. Divide the cooked bacon slices equally among the cheese-spread slices of bread and top the cheese with the bacon slices (about two slices per sandwich). Top the bacon with four thin tomato slices. Close the sandwiches with the eight plain slices of bread. Brush the outside of each sandwich with melted butter or spray with olive oil cooking spray.

Cook in a panini or other sandwich press. Or cook in a nonstick sauté pan: Weight the sandwich with a cake pan holding a 28-ounce can. Cook on one side until golden brown, remove the weight, turn the sandwich, and cook on the second side until golden brown and the cheese melts.

Slice the sandwich in half and serve with soup or chips.

### VARIATION
Substitute 4 cups of prepared pimiento cheese for homemade cheese.

# Brat and Swiss Cheese Panini

**Serves 8**

*At the Berghoff we use bratwurst and Swiss cheese in many different dishes—entrées, sandwiches, soups, appetizers, sides, and even pizzas. So, of course, we have a panini option. You can purchase Swiss cheese in one-ounce slices, or one pound of thinly sliced Swiss cheese.*

16 slices Berghoff Sandwich Rye
(page 46), or purchased rye bread

½ cup brown mustard

32 (1-ounce) slices Swiss cheese, or
1 pound thinly sliced Swiss cheese

8 fully cooked (6-inch) bratwurst,
sliced thinly on the diagonal

Melted butter or nonstick cooking spray

Spread eight slices of bread with 1 tablespoon of mustard. Place one 1-ounce slice of Swiss cheese on eight of the slices of bread. (Or if using thinly sliced Swiss cheese, divide the cheese into eight equal portions and place ½ portion on each of the eight slices of bread.) Divide the sausage into eight portions and distribute evenly on the eight cheese-topped bread slices. Top the sausage with the remaining Swiss cheese. Close the sandwiches with the remaining eight slices of bread. Brush the outsides of each sandwich with melted butter or spray with cooking spray.

Cook in a panini or other sandwich press. Or cook in a nonstick sauté pan: Weight each sandwich with a cake pan holding a 28-ounce can. Cook on one side until golden brown, remove the weight, turn the sandwich, and cook on the second side until golden brown and the cheese melts.

Slice each sandwich in half and serve with soup or chips.

# The "Patini" Bar

I cook at home with my kids every chance I get. One day, my young son Todd got too hungry to wait for dinner. So we opened the fridge to see what we could find to keep starvation at bay: tomatoes, spinach, cheese, sliced ham, bread, and more interesting bits and pieces. "Let's make patinis!" he said. "You mean panini?" "Yes," he said, "patinis!"

So we took everything out of the fridge and laid it out on the counter, bread first, right up to where we set the panini grill. And that is how I developed the layout for a perfect panini bar. Oh, yes, and we made some great patinis. Lay out your choice of ingredients in the order that follows:

1. Sliced breads
White, wheat, challah, multigrain, rye, pumpernickel, English muffins

2. Spreads for the inside of the bread
Butter, mayonnaise, mustards, olive oil, fruit chutneys, jams, tapenade, peanut butter

3. Sliced or shredded cheeses
Soft (Brie-type, plain and flavored cream cheeses), smoked, Cheddars, Swiss, blue, Jack, brick, Muenster

4. Sliced cooked meats, poultry, fish
Beef, ham, pork, chicken, turkey, salami and cured sausages, smoked salmon, smoked or barbecued meats

5. Thinly sliced fresh, cooked or canned vegetables, fruits, and greens

6. Cooking sprays or a dish of olive oil with brush for outside of the bread

7. The panini grill itself

You don't even need a panini grill. Just fire up the stove to medium, put on a good nonstick skillet sprayed with cooking spray, put in the panini one at a time, and weight each down with a flat-bottomed cake pan holding a 28-ounce can.

# Today Panini, Yesterday Grilled Cheese

Today's panini is yesterday's grilled cheese sandwich with an Italian accent. Grilled cheese sandwiches probably appeared in the 1930s when sliced white bread, inexpensive processed American cheese, and electric sandwich makers were popular items. (The bread slicer was patented in 1928 and sliced white bread hit the market July 7 of that year. James L. Kraft got the first patent for processed cheese in 1916, sold six million pounds to the U.S. military during World War I, and then captured the consumer market. The first electric sandwich maker was invented in the 1920s by Charles Champion.) Panini (plural of panino) were originally Italian and served in panintecas (sandwich shops) in Italy. In the 1970s, Americans took notice and panini started appearing in upscale eateries. By the 1990s, panini were firmly installed in college and hospital cafeterias, airport food courts, and family restaurants—like the Berghoff Café.

# Westphalian Ham Panini with Granny Smith Apple and Applesauce

**Serves 8**

*"Fromage de Brie" was on the 1914 café menu, but my twist on that tradition is to add thinly sliced apples and applesauce and some Westphalian ham. I use homemade applesauce, but any good applesauce from the jar works just as well.*

16 slices sourdough bread

¾ cup brown mustard

12 ounces (¾ pound) Brie, cut into eight equal pieces

24 paper-thin cored, peeled Granny Smith apple slices (2 to 3 apples)

½ cup homemade Applesauce (page 83), or prepared applesauce

16 thin slices Westphalian ham

Melted butter, as needed, or olive oil nonstick cooking spray

Spread each slice of bread with 2 teaspoons of mustard. On eight of the bread slices, spread evenly one portion of Brie, top with three apple slices, 1 tablespoon of applesauce, and two slices of ham. Top each with a second slice of bread, mustard side down. Brush the outside of each sandwich with melted butter or spray with olive oil cooking spray.

Cook in a panini or other sandwich press. Or cook in a nonstick sauté pan: Weight each sandwich with a cake pan holding a 28-ounce can. Cook on one side until golden brown, remove the weight, turn the sandwich, and cook on the second side until golden brown and the cheese melts.

Slice the sandwich in half and serve with soup or chips.

# All-Day, All-Night Fried Egg Sandwich

**Serves 8**

*It's no wonder egg sandwiches have been American classics since the early 1900s in diners and in family and fast-food restaurants. They are easy-to-make, satisfying, hot meals that can be eaten at any time of the day or night. At the café, we make ours to order—soft, medium, or hard yolk—on plain Berghoff Sandwich Rye, or traditional sliced white sandwich bread. At home I sometimes use lightly toasted English muffins or sliced challah.*

16 (½-inch-thick) slices good
white sandwich bread, or Berghoff
Sandwich Rye (page 46), toasted

½ pound thinly sliced Westphalian
ham at room temperature

8 tablespoons unsalted butter

16 large eggs

Kosher salt and freshly ground
black pepper

Divide the ham into eight equal portions. Place one portion on each of eight slices of the toasted bread.

In a large nonstick skillet over medium heat, melt 1 tablespoon of the butter. Crack two of the eggs into a cup and slide neatly into the pan. Cook the eggs for 3 minutes, then place 1 scant tablespoon of water into the skillet lid (not in the skillet) and cover the skillet. Let cook to desired degree of doneness, about 30 seconds, covered, for a soft yolk; 1 minute, covered, for medium. Add salt and pepper to taste.

As each pair of eggs is cooked, slide, along with the cooking butter in the pan, onto the ham. Place a second slice of toast on top.
Serve on a plate, but do not slice. Repeat with the remaining butter, eggs, and bread.

Serve with a knife and fork.

## VARIATIONS

Substitute toasted sliced challah or English muffins for the white or rye bread.

Sauté the ham lightly in the nonstick skillet before you cook the eggs to brown and crisp it.

# Berghoff Sandwich Rye

**Makes 1 large loaf**

*I created this recipe especially for sandwiches. It's easy to make—in a bowl, food processor, or standing mixer—and comes in three flavors: dill seed, bacon and onion, and sauerkraut. It also makes great toast. Be sure to use quick-rising or instant active dry yeast. You can mix it right in with the flour, and the dough rises faster. Our bread baker, Enrique Sta Marie ("Bong" to us), always weighs flour, rather than measures. Flour settles, so one measured cup of packed flour is more than one measured cup fluffed. I always put the flour in a big bowl, then fluff it with a large spoon to aerate it. Then I scoop a cup and level the top. That way my one cup is always the same.*

2½ cups unbleached all-purpose flour, fluffed, scooped, leveled, plus additional as needed

1½ cups medium rye flour, fluffed, scooped, and leveled (see Notes)

1 tablespoon sugar

1½ teaspoons salt

1 (¼-ounce) package (2¼ teaspoons) quick-rising (instant) dry active yeast

1 rounded tablespoon dill seeds

1½ cups warm water (110°F), plus more if needed (see Notes)

2 tablespoons canola oil

Vegetable oil cooking spray

To mix by hand: In a 4-quart bowl, combine the flours, sugar, salt, yeast, and dill seeds. Stir to mix. Add the water and oil. Mix with a large spoon until the dough pulls away from the sides of the bowl. If the dough is too stiff or dry, add water by the tablespoon, until the dough is soft enough to knead. Then knead it directly in the bowl, adding more flour as necessary, until smooth and elastic, 8 to 10 minutes.

Spray the top of the dough with cooking spray. Cover the bowl with plastic wrap. Let rise in a warm place (75° to 85°F) until doubled, 1 hour to 1 hour 15 minutes.

To mix in a food processor: In the work bowl of a large-capacity (14-cup) food processor fitted with the plastic blade, combine all the dry ingredients. Put on the lid and pulse to mix. With the motor running, pour the water and oil through the feed tube and process just until the dough pulls away from the side of the bowl, about 2 minutes. If the dough is too stiff, add more water by the tablespoon until the dough forms a smooth, cohesive mass. Remove the dough from the food processor and knead briefly, just to shape, on a lightly floured surface.

Spray a large bowl with cooking spray, place the dough in it, and spray the top of the dough. Cover the bowl with plastic wrap and let rise in a warm place until doubled, 1 hour to 1 hour 15 minutes.

To mix in a standing mixer: In the bowl of a standing mixer fitted with the paddle attachment, combine all the dry ingredients. Stir to mix. With the motor on slow speed, pour in the water and oil. Let the machine mix the ingredients until a rough dough forms. Remove the paddle and scrape it down. Fit the machine with the dough hook and let the machine knead the dough until the dough pulls away from the side of the bowl and is smooth and elastic, 8 to 10 minutes, adding water by the tablespoon if the dough is too stiff, or flour by the tablespoon if the dough is too wet. As needed, stop the machine to scrape down the sides and bottom with a plastic spatula. Remove the dough hook, and remove the dough from the bowl.

Spray the mixer bowl (no need to wash) with cooking spray, place the dough back in, and spray the top of the dough. Cover the bowl with plastic wrap and let rise in a warm place until doubled, 1 hour to 1 hour 15 minutes.

To shape and bake: Preheat the oven to 375°F. Turn out the fully risen dough onto a lightly floured surface. Punch down, knead briefly, and shape into a loaf. Place in a 9 by 5 by 2½-inch loaf pan that has been well sprayed with cooking spray. Spray the top of the dough. Cover loosely with parchment paper, waxed paper, or a clean, lint-free kitchen towel that has been wetted and wrung out. Let rise in a warm place until doubled, about 1 hour. Bake until golden brown and the loaf sounds hollow when tapped, 35 to 40 minutes.

Remove the pan from the oven. To ensure the baked bread comes out easily from the pan, run a thin-bladed cake spatula around all four edges of the loaf pan. Remove the bread from the pan and let cool to room temperature on a wire rack.

## VARIATIONS

For sauerkraut rye: Add to the flour mixture one 14-ounce can of sauerkraut, preferably Bavarian style, drained and squeezed dry. Follow the recipe directions for mixing, kneading, and baking. Omit the dill seeds if desired.

For bacon and onion rye: Decrease the salt to 1 teaspoon and add to the flour mixture 2 tablespoons of bacon bits (from a jar) and 2 tablespoons of dried minced onion. Follow the recipe directions for mixing, kneading, and baking. Omit the dill seeds if desired.

For plain rye: Omit the dill seeds.

*Notes:* Rye flour is not as popular today as in decades past, so I order mine online. I use medium rye because it makes a nice, light loaf but still has a distinct rye flavor. Medium rye has the germ and some of the bran removed. There is also white rye, which has all the germ and bran removed and makes a light loaf with less rye flavor. At the other extreme, there is pumpernickel flour, which contains all the germ and bran. It makes a flavorful but dense loaf.

Always use cold, fresh tap water. Heat it to 110°F in a microwave for about 15 seconds or on the stovetop.

To test for proper rising, after the dough has risen, using two fingers, press down about ½ inch on top. If the indentation remains, the dough has fully risen. If the dough springs back leaving no indentation, let it rise longer.

## THE CLUB HOUSE SANDWICH

There are at least three histories of the original club house sandwich, which consisted of cooked chicken breast, bacon, sliced tomatoes, and crisp lettuce layered between two—or three—slices of bread. One version is that in 1894, the club sandwich was created in the kitchen of the Saratoga Club-House, Saratoga Springs, New York. A second version is that it was created by an anonymous very hungry man who came home late and, while making himself some toast, searched the pantry—he found bacon, cold chicken, tomato, lettuce, and mayonnaise—and put these leftovers between his toast. Yet a third version suggests it was a two-decker sandwich that originated aboard double-decker club cars traveling between New York and Chicago in the 1930s and '40s. And the late James Beard added his two cents, declaring that the two-decker original club house sandwich was one of the great sandwiches of all times—but that a three-decker was a horror.

# Club House Sandwich

**Serves 8**

*At the café, chef Matt Reichel apparently agrees with the late James Beard that the best club house sandwich has only two, not three, slices of bread. We make ours with sliced turkey (which also stars in our Turkey Reuben and Turkey Okra Soup). You can roast your own turkey breast as we do or buy good sliced turkey breast from the deli.*

16 (½-inch thick) slices good white sandwich bread, toasted or untoasted

8 tablespoons mayonnaise

16 leaves iceberg, Bibb, or Boston lettuce

1½ pounds thinly sliced, roasted turkey breast (page 54)

16 thin slices ripe tomato

1 pound (16 strips) crisp, cooked bacon

8 (1-ounce) slices Swiss cheese

Lay out the bread on a clean, dry surface. Spread each of eight slices with 1 tablespoon of mayonnaise. Top each with two lettuce leaves. Divide the sliced turkey into eight equal portions. Top the lettuce with one portion of turkey. Top the turkey with two slices of tomato, then two strips of bacon, and two slices of cheese. Top each with the remaining eight slices of bread. Press down gently to hold. Slice in half and secure each half with a toothpick. Serve with potato chips.

**VARIATIONS**

Substitute challah for the sandwich bread.

Use ½ pound of very thinly sliced Swiss cheese divided into eight equal portions.

# Hamburger with Beer-Braised Onions

**Serves 8**

*Our café burgers are big and juicy and one of our biggest sellers year-round. We shape the patties from freshly ground prime Black Angus beef that is 80 to 85 percent lean. Is it the burger or the onions that makes it so special? You decide.*

5 pounds ground Black Angus beef sirloin

1 teaspoon kosher salt

1 teaspoon freshly ground black pepper

16 slices aged Cheddar cheese (optional)

8 kaiser rolls, sliced in half

16 leaves iceberg, leaf, or Bibb lettuce

2 cups Beer-Braised Onions (page 51)

16 thin slices ripe tomato

½ cup prepared barbecue sauce

16 slices applewood-smoked bacon, crisply cooked

In a large bowl, combine the ground beef, salt, and pepper. Using a large spoon or rubber spatula, mix well. Divide the mixture into eight equal portions. Place a bowl of cold water next to the bowl with the meat and place your hands in the cold water before you shape each patty, to keep the meat from sticking. Shape the meat into eight patties no more than ½ inch thick. Place the shaped burgers on a parchment paper or waxed paper–lined cookie sheet.

Cook on an outdoor or indoor grill, turning once, to an internal temperature of 165°F, measured on an instant-read meat thermometer. Or cook, no more than three burgers at a time, in a 12-inch nonstick skillet lightly sprayed with nonstick cooking spray, to an internal temperature of 165°F, turning once. During the last 2 minutes of cooking, top each burger with two slices of cheese, if using, and finish cooking until the cheese melts.

For each burger, place two lettuce leaves, ¼ cup of beer-braised onions, and two tomato slices on each bun bottom. Spread with 1 tablespoon of barbecue sauce. Top with the cooked burger and two slices of bacon. Cover with the top half of bun. Serve with potato chips.

**VARIATIONS**

Substitute Swiss, provolone, or Gouda cheese for the Cheddar.

Substitute ground turkey for the beef.

# Beer-Braised Onions

**Makes 2 cups**

*The thinner the onions are sliced, the quicker they brown and the more readily they absorb the beer. At the café, chef Matt Reichel uses a large mandoline to slice ten-pound bags of onions paper thin. At home, I use a small, inexpensive Japanese-made mandoline and get the same results—with a much smaller quantity of onions. But you can also just slice the onions as thinly as possible, about ⅛ inch thick. And you can double this recipe.*

**2 tablespoons oil**

**3 cups thinly sliced yellow onion, packed**

**¾ cup Berghoff amber beer**

**Kosher salt and pepper**

Heat the oil in an 8- to 10-inch sauté pan over medium heat. Add the onion and cook, stirring occasionally, until golden brown, 10 to 15 minutes. Add the beer and salt and pepper and simmer, stirring often, until the liquid has almost evaporated and the onions are golden brown, about 15 minutes. Season to taste. Remove from the heat and keep warm.

# Turkey Reuben

**Serves 8**

*The Berghoff Café Turkey Reuben is a year-round favorite that customers love. It is made with our own Roasted Herb-Marinated Turkey Breast, our own Thousand Island Dressing, and our signature sauerkraut. You may substitute sliced turkey from the deli, but if you roast your own you can also use it in the Club House Sandwich (page 49) and in Turkey, Okra, and Rice Soup (page 34).*

16 slices Berghoff Sandwich Rye bread, any variation (page 46)

16 slices Swiss cheese

2⅔ cups rinsed, well-drained sauerkraut

¾ cup Café Thousand Island Dressing (page 78) or prepared Thousand Island dressing

2 pounds thinly sliced Roasted Herb-Marinated Turkey Breast (page 54) or sliced turkey breast from the deli

Melted butter or nonstick cooking spray

8 dill pickle spears, for garnish

For each sandwich: Lay one slice of bread on a clean surface. Top with one slice of cheese. Divide the sliced turkey into eight equal portions and lay one portion on top of the cheese. Top the turkey with ⅓ cup of the sauerkraut. Spread 1½ tablespoons of dressing over the sauerkraut. Top with one slice of cheese. Place a second slice of bread on top to complete the sandwich. Press gently to hold together. Repeat with the remaining ingredients to make a total of eight sandwiches. Place on a baking tray, cover with plastic wrap, and refrigerate until ready to cook.

To cook: Brush each sandwich on both sides with butter or spray with cooking spray. Cook in a panini or other sandwich press. Or cook in a nonstick sauté pan: Weight the sandwich with a cake pan holding a 28-ounce can. Cook on one side until golden brown, remove the weight, turn the sandwich, and cook on the second side until golden brown and the cheese melts.

Serve hot, with each sandwich accompanied by a dill pickle spear.

## VARIATIONS

Substitute prepared purchased rye bread for the Berghoff Sandwich Rye.

Substitute Berghoff Coleslaw or prepared cole-slaw from the deli for the sauerkraut.

# Roasted Herb-Marinated Turkey Breast

**Makes one 5- to 7–pound turkey breast**

*This couldn't be easier to roast, and you will have enough turkey for sandwiches, soup, and even dinner.*

1 (5- to 7-pound) boneless turkey breast

¼ cup finely diced shallots

2 tablespoons olive oil

1 ½ tablespoons chopped fresh thyme

1 tablespoon chopped fresh marjoram

1 tablespoon minced fresh garlic

1 teaspoon kosher salt

½ teaspoon freshly ground black pepper

Rinse the turkey breast and pat dry. Place in a large resealable plastic bag and refrigerate until ready to marinate.

In a 1-quart bowl, combine the remaining ingredients. Cover and let stand for 1 hour. Remove the turkey breast from the refrigerator. Open the bag, pour the marinade over the turkey, and reseal the bag, removing as much air as possible. Turn the bag several times to coat the turkey well with the marinade. Place on a tray and refrigerate for 4 to 6 hours or overnight, turning often.

To cook: Remove the turkey breast from the bag; discard the bag and the marinade. Preheat the oven to 325°F. Place the turkey breast in a roasting pan and cook until the internal temperature (as registered on an instant-read meat thermometer) reaches 160°F, 1 to 1½ hours. Remove the pan from the oven. Cover loosely with foil and let rest for 10 to 15 minutes before slicing.

# Corned Beef Sandwich

**Serves 8**

*This recipe appears in* The Berghoff Family Cookbook. *It was one of Great-grandfather Herman's first café sandwiches served in 1898. And in it we share our family secret for moist corned beef. My only twist on this tradition is to serve the sandwich on Berghoff Sandwich Rye.*

5 pounds lean, uncooked corned beef

1 tablespoon pickling spice

4 quarts water, or enough
to cover the meat

Salt and pepper

½ cup Dijon or Dusseldorf mustard

16 slices Berghoff Sandwich rye,
any variation (page 46)

In a pot large enough to hold all the meat, place the corned beef, picking spice, and water. Make certain the water completely covers the meat. Bring the mixture to a boil, then decrease the heat and let the meat simmer, covered, for 2½ to 3 hours. Insert a fork into the meat and it should pull out easily when done. Remove the meat from the pot and let it cool, reserving the cooking liquid. Refrigerate the meat and liquid until completely cool, 3 to 4 hours.

After the meat has cooled, remove and discard the fat. Slice the meat about ¹⁄₁₆ inch thick with the grain, on a slight angle. This should yield eight 5- to 6-ounce portions of meat for each sandwich.

Remove and discard any solid fat from the reserved cooking liquid. Reheat the cooking liquid to a boil; decrease the heat to a simmer and season with salt and pepper. Dip the meat in batches into the liquid, using a heatproof strainer or small colander. Remove and let drain for 1 minute.

Make eight sandwiches, distributing the corned beef among eight slices of rye bread spread with mustard, and topping each with another slice of rye bread. Cut in half to serve.

**VARIATION**
Substitute your favorite rye bread for Berghoff Sandwich Rye.

# Berghoff Sub

**Serves 8**

*Sometimes called a hoagie, a hero, or a grinder, the submarine sandwich appeared in Italian-American communities in the northeastern United States in the late nineteenth century but spread from there all over the country. Our café version is a meal in itself, great for lunch, picnics, Super Bowl parties, or brown-bagging it at the office. We slice the bun in half but not all the way through, so the bun opens and closes on its own "hinge."*

*Also, chef Matt Reichel roasts his own red bell peppers and peels them—adding great flavor.*

1 pound thinly sliced Genoa salami

1 pound thinly sliced provolone cheese

1 pound thinly sliced capicola sausage

4 cups shredded iceberg lettuce

2 cups drained, jarred roasted red peppers, chopped coarsely

8 green pickled pepperoncini, stemmed, sliced thinly

24 paper-thin slices ripe tomato

1 red onion, sliced paper thin

8 (8-inch) long baguettes or French rolls, sliced to hinge

¼ cup prepared Italian dressing

Divide the salami, cheese, capicola, iceberg, red peppers, pepperoncini, tomato slices, and sliced red onion into eight equal portions and place on a cutting board or baking tray. On the bottom half of each baguette or roll, layer one portion of each, starting with the salami and ending with the red onion. Drizzle each sandwich filling with 2 teaspoons of Italian dressing. Close the top of the baguette or roll over the filling and press gently to hold.

Cut in half and secure each half with a wooden toothpick. Serve with chips or apple wedges.

### VARIATION

If you like more Italian dressing, increase the amount to 1 tablespoon per sandwich or ½ cup for the whole recipe.

# The Real Thing Frankfurter

**Serves 8**

*The key to this great simple sandwich is to use real, natural-casing frankfurters, not the hot dogs widely available in supermarkets. There is a world of difference in texture and taste. You can purchase frankfurters online and at butcher shops. Buy fully cooked frankfurters, and cook to heat through by simmering in water or beer, or by grilling.*

**8 fully cooked, natural-casing frankfurters**

**16 slices Berghoff Sandwich Rye with dill seed (page 46)**

**½ cup brown mustard**

In a 12-inch sauté pan, place the frankfurters in a single layer. Cover with water or Berghoff amber beer. Bring to a simmer. Simmer until heated through, 5 to 8 minutes. Remove with tongs to a cutting board. Alternatively, grill on an outdoor or indoor grill for 8 to 10 minutes, turning often.

Spread each slice of bread with 1½ teaspoons of the mustard. Slice the frankfurters in half lengthwise. Place both halves of one frankfurter, cut side down, diagonally on one slice of bread. Top with a second slice of bread. Cut the sandwich in half diagonally in the opposite direction. Serve with potato chips, a scoop of coleslaw, or a spoonful of your favorite prepared sauerkraut.

**VARIATION**

Substitute your favorite rye bread or white sandwich bread for the Berghoff Sandwich Rye.

## CRUMBS AND CROUTONS

Grandmother Carlyn never threw bread away. Instead, she turned it into soft and dry crumbs and croutons. She used the soft bread crumbs, sautéed in butter until golden (poor man's Parmesan), to top boiled noodles and casseroles of every kind before baking. She used the dried bread crumbs for inside apple strudel, and to line buttered casserole and soufflé dishes before filling and baking. She would even add sugar, cinnamon, and butter and use them as a sweet crust for cheesecakes and icebox cakes and pies. With today's food processors, crumbs are easier than ever. For soft crumbs, tear bread, crusts and all, into small pieces and pulse until crumbs are formed. For dried bread crumbs, tear the bread and spread on a baking tray to dry. Then pulse until the crumbs are formed. For soft croutons, cut the bread into cubes, then sauté in butter or olive oil, until golden on all sides. For dry croutons, bake the cubes at 300°F until golden, about 20 minutes. Store the crumbs and croutons in resealable plastic bags, label, and freeze for up to 30 days.

# CHAPTER 4

## SALADS

# To Make the Meal

Some of the café's salads have been around since 1914: lobster, shrimp, coleslaw, cucumbers, and potato salad. But today, some of our most popular salads that depend on fresh mixed lettuces, such as Asian Chicken Salad (page 64) would come as a big surprise to Great-grandad.

Until the 1920s, fresh lettuce was mostly seasonal and from the garden. Lettuce was highly perishable and almost impossible to ship long distances, even from California, where it grows year-round. But in 1926, a hardy variety of head lettuce called crisp-head lettuce—today's iceberg lettuce—was first shipped in ice by railroad cars from California all over the country.

The only two salads my grand-mother Carlyn ever served were iceberg lettuce leaves with sliced tomato in season and her crisp buttery croutons, and second, a wedge of iceberg lettuce with Roquefort cheese dressing. It would also explain why there was one lettuce salad on the 1932 Berghoff menu (simply listed as "Lettuce, 20 cents"). The real

greening of the Berghoff came when my mom, Jan, took over the menu in 1986. She and the chef created several salads made with a variety of greens, including fresh spinach, and those salads were a sellout. Today our salads are more than 50 percent of our café sales. Most of these are not side salads; they're big and bountiful and make the meal for many customers.

My children eat a wide variety of vegetables, mostly raw. That's because of our home salad bar. Each of the children gets a bowl of finely chopped romaine hearts and Bibb lettuce and can choose which vegetables to top it with. A typical spread would be thinly sliced or chopped carrots, celery, bell peppers, cucumbers, tomatoes, shredded cheese, and olives. Their favorite dressing is ranch.

As a kid, I liked my grandmother's sweet vinaigrette. She mixed and stored it in a clean pickle jar with a lid. When it was time to serve it, she just gave it a good shake. I make a very basic ranch dressing for my kids the same way in a quart mason jar with a lid, and store it in the fridge.

I have always believed in making salad dressings from scratch. They are easy to mix, and vinegar- and oil-based dressings keep well refrigerated for up to two weeks. Homemade dressings are much less expensive than bottled dressings, and many of the salad dressings in this chapter can do double duty as spreads or dips.

Some of our customer's favorite main-dish salads, including Berghoff Buffalo Cobb, are good not only as main-dish salads for lunch and light supper but they make great buffet dishes as well.

# Iceberg Wedge with Roquefort Dressing and Bacon

**Serves 8**

*Grandmother Carlyn served this salad almost every Sunday. We never got tired of it, and the whole family loves it still. My twist is to add tiny red tomatoes and some shredded Parmesan for extra color and flavor. One tip for crisp iceberg lettuce: Core the lettuce head and rinse upside down under lots of cold running water. Remove any wilted outer leaves and discard. Then line a bowl with several thicknesses of paper toweling, set the lettuce in right side up, cover the bowl with plastic wrap, and refrigerate until ready to cut into wedges.*

8 iceberg lettuce wedges (2 heads)

2½ cups crumbled Roquefort cheese

32 teardrop tomatoes, halved

1 cup shredded Parmesan cheese

8 slices crisp, cooked bacon

2 cups Roquefort Cheese Dressing (page 72)

For each salad: Lay one iceberg wedge on a chilled plate, cut side up. Sprinkle the wedge with ¼ cup of crumbled Roquefort. Distribute eight tomato halves around the wedge. Sprinkle 2 tablespoons of Parmesan on top of the wedge, and lay one bacon strip on top either whole or crumbled. Drizzle ¼ cup of Roquefort dressing over the wedge and serve immediately.

**VARIATIONS**

Substitute grape or cherry tomatoes for teardrop.

Substitute prepared bottled Roquefort dressing for homemade.

Increase the Roquefort dressing to ⅓ cup if you like a lot of dressing.

For a vegetarian version, omit the bacon.

## THE ICEBERGS ARE COMING!

In 1926, Bruce Church, founder of Fresh Express, today's popular produce line, started shipping the hardy variety of lettuce called crisphead lettuce from Salinas, California, all the way to the East Coast. He loaded the heads of lettuce in railroad boxcars and covered them with ice. When the trains passed into towns along the way, people would shout, "The icebergs are coming!"

# Berghoff Buffalo Cobb

**Serves 8**

*The flavor of roasted (actually broiled) corn adds a lot to our café's popular main-dish salad, as does the freshly grilled chicken breast. But when I run out of time at home, I often substitute leftover chicken and cooked canned or frozen corn kernels. In the summertime, I grill fresh ears of corn on the outdoor grill, then cut them off the cob for the salad.*

2 cups corn kernels

1 tablespoon canola oil

2 pounds Grilled Chicken Breast, cut into strips (page 65)

1 cup prepared barbecue sauce

1 (28-ounce) or 2 (15-ounce) cans kidney beans, rinsed and drained

2 cups peeled, diced, seedless cucumber

2 cups diced fresh tomato

8 cups chopped romaine lettuce

1 cup Ranch Dressing (page 79)

2 large ripe avocados

Canned fried onions, for garnish

To roast the corn: Preheat the broiler to 500°F. In a small bowl, toss 2 cups of the corn with the canola oil. Spread the corn on a sheet pan and cook under the broiler until browned, turning once or twice with a spatula, about 5 minutes. Let cool to room temperature.

In a medium-size bowl, toss the grilled chicken strips and barbecue sauce and set aside. In a large bowl, gently toss together the corn, kidney beans, cucumber, tomato, and romaine. Add the Ranch Dressing and toss to cover. Divide among eight individual serving plates. Just before serving, peel, pit, and dice the avocados. In the center of each serving, place ⅔ cup of the sauced chicken and sprinkle one-eighth of the avocado pieces over the chicken. Garnish with the fried onions.

## VARIATIONS

Substitute cooked, drained frozen or canned corn kernels for roasted.

Substitute prepared ranch dressing for homemade.

Substitute any cooked chicken for grilled.

# Asian Chicken Salad

**Serves 8**

*This is one of the café's most popular main-dish salads. We make ours with cooked soba (Japanese buckwheat) noodles, which are available today in supermarkets and come in various sizes; the most common are eight- and twelve-ounce packages. Or you can also use cooked spaghetti. One pound of dry spaghetti or soba yields eight cups of cooked noodles. Cook the soba in lightly salted boiling water according to the package directions. It's important to rinse both the cooked spaghetti and soba under cold water and drain very well before using in this salad.*

2 pounds boneless, skinless grilled chicken breasts, shredded (page 65)

8 cups ready-to-use baby lettuce

1 pound cooked, rinsed, drained spaghetti or soba noodles (8 cups)

4 cups shredded green cabbage

2 cups seeded and julienned red bell pepper

2 cups seeded and julienned yellow bell pepper

2 cups shredded carrots

1 cup thinly sliced seedless cucumber

½ pound fresh snow peas

2 cups drained canned mandarin orange segments

1 cup Peanut Butter Dressing (page 75)

1 (14-ounce) can crisp chow mein noodles, for garnish

In a large bowl mix together all the ingredients except the dressing and chow mein noodles. Toss well with the dressing to coat.

To serve: Divide into eight servings, and garnish each with chow mein noodles. Serve extra dressing on the side if desired.

**VARIATION**

Substitute any leftover cooked chicken breast for freshly grilled.

# Grilled Chicken Breast

**Makes 2 pounds**

*I like to hand-pull cooked chicken and turkey into shreds rather than slice it. It enhances the texture and allows the chicken to absorb flavors more readily.*

¼ **cup dry sherry**

½ **cup prepared teriyaki sauce**

2 **pounds boneless, skinless chicken breasts**

In a glass bowl, mix together the sherry, teriyaki sauce, and chicken. Cover and refrigerate, turning occasionally, for 1 hour. Preheat the grill. Remove the chicken from the marinade, discard the marinade, and grill the chicken until cooked through to an internal temperature of 165°F, measured by an instant-read meat thermometer. Remove from the grill and let rest for 15 minutes. Either shred by hand, wearing disposable plastic gloves, or by pulling the meat into shreds with a fork. You may also slice into julienne strips.

**VARIATION**

Instead of grilling, you can also sauté the chicken in a 12-inch nonstick sauté pan over medium heat, turning once, to an internal temperature of 165°F, measured by an instant-read meat thermometer.

# Shrimp Salad with Thousand Island Dressing

**Serves 8**

*This is a flavorful, pretty, main-dish shrimp salad. We like to grill or sauté our shrimp in a little olive oil until just cooked to ensure the perfect texture—the shrimp shouldn't be soft and mushy. At home I would purchase a two-pound bag of frozen, raw, shelled, deveined, tail-on shrimp, either 21/25 or 16/20 (shrimp to the pound). Don't cook it frozen, which will toughen it. Either thaw the bag overnight in the refrigerator, or open the bag and place the shrimp in a big bowl of cold water until thawed, 5 to 10 minutes, then drain.*

2 pounds frozen 21/25 or 16/20 shelled, deveined, tail-on raw shrimp

Olive oil

Kosher salt and freshly ground black pepper

1 cup diced celery

1 cup chopped green onion, white and green parts

1 cup chopped tomato, fresh or canned, drained

1 cup drained, diced pimientos

1½ cups Café Thousand Island Dressing (page 78)

2 quarts butter lettuce leaves

4 red bell peppers, cored, seeded, and halved lengthwise

Minced green onion, for garnish

Thaw the frozen shrimp and remove and discard the tails. Drain well and pat dry with paper toweling. Heat 1 tablespoon of olive oil in a 12-inch nonstick skillet over medium heat. Add the shrimp in batches and sauté, stirring, until just cooked through. Transfer the cooked shrimp to a baking sheet. Repeat, using additional oil as needed, until all the shrimp are cooked. Season very lightly with salt and pepper. Let cool to room temperature, then chop the shrimp into ½-inch pieces. Transfer the shrimp and any juices to a 2-quart bowl. Add the celery, green onion, tomato, and pimientos, and toss to mix.

Divide this mixture in half. Place half in one bowl, cover with plastic wrap, and refrigerate for at least 2 hours before serving. Mix the second half of the shrimp mixture with the thousand island dressing, tossing well to mix. Cover with plastic wrap and refrigerate for at least 2 hours before serving.

To serve: Divide the lettuce into eight portions and spread each portion on a large, chilled plate. Place one hollow red pepper half in the middle. Fill the pepper with one-eighth of the dressing-coated shrimp mixture. Sprinkle one-eighth of the undressed shrimp mixture on top of the lettuce around the pepper. Garnish with the minced green onion.

## VARIATION

Omit the red pepper halves and scoop 1 mounded cup of the dressing-coated shrimp mixture in the middle of the bed of lettuce, then sprinkle the undressed shrimp mixture around the edges.

# Coleslaw

**Serves 8**

*Coleslaw, or some form of shredded raw cabbage with dressing, has been eaten since ancient Rome. But coleslaw as we know it, and as the café first served it, made with mayonnaise dressing, was not invented until the eighteenth century—when mayonnaise first made its appearance. This is the original Berghoff Café recipe from 1914. It keeps, refrigerated, up to four days and only gets better with age.*

¾ **cup mayonnaise**

3 **tablespoons apple cider vinegar**

2 **tablespoons sugar**

2 **tablespoons Dijon mustard**

1 **pound finely shredded green cabbage**

1 **cup finely shredded carrots**

1 **cup finely shredded red cabbage**

**Kosher salt and freshly ground black pepper**

In a 4-quart bowl, whisk together the mayonnaise, vinegar, sugar and Dijon until the sugar dissolves. Add the green cabbage, carrots, and red cabbage. Toss until well mixed and coated with the dressing. Season to taste with salt and pepper. Cover with plastic wrap or a lid and chill for at least 2 hours before serving.

# New Potato Salad with Dill

**Serves 8**

*This is a side salad, not a main dish. It goes very well with sandwiches, and makes a nice side dish for grilled poultry, meats, and fish. It's a good make-ahead buffet dish. And if you are cooking for vegetarians, such as my daughter Sarah, just add grilled vegetables or a grilled cheese panino.*

2 pounds unpeeled red potatoes

1 teaspoon salt

1½ cups light mayonnaise

¼ cup light sour cream

¼ cup red wine vinegar

½ cup diced celery

½ cup diced yellow onion

1 tablespoon finely chopped fresh dill

Kosher salt and freshly ground black pepper

Place the potatoes in a 3-quart pot and cover with 1 inch of water. Add the salt. Bring to a boil over medium heat. Decrease the heat and cook until tender but not mushy when tested with a fork, about 25 minutes. Remove from the heat and drain in a colander. Let cool to room temperature and then cut into cubes.

In a 4-quart bowl, whisk together the mayonnaise, sour cream, and vinegar. Fold in the cubed potatoes, celery, onion, and dill. Toss to mix well and coat with the dressing. Season to taste. Cover with plastic wrap or a lid and refrigerate for at least 2 hours before serving.

# Pear Salad with Greens, Candied Walnuts, and Sun-Dried Cherries

**Serves 8**

*This salad has a lot of textures, flavors, and colors. And because of the fresh pears, we make it individually, to order. We serve it in the café as a side dish to go with almost any soup, sandwich, or grilled main dish. But some customers love it so much, they order a double portion and eat it as a main-dish salad. You can do the same by doubling the recipe. Candied nuts are available in supermarkets and gourmet stores.*

3 quarts mixed ready-to-use salad greens

1 cup Champagne Vinaigrette (page 73)

2 cups crumbled Roquefort cheese

1 cup sun-dried cherries

4 unpeeled pears, cored, and sliced into 12 slices each

1 cup prepared candied walnuts, pecans, or almonds

For each salad, in a large bowl, toss together 1½ cups of the greens with 2 tablespoons of the dressing. Add 2 tablespoons each of the Roquefort crumbles and cherries, and toss again. Place the mixture on a chilled plate and arrange six pear slices around the salad. Sprinkle the top with 2 tablespoons of candied nuts. Repeat for the other salads. Serve immediately.

### VARIATION

Substitute Candied Peanuts, Sweet Asian Peanuts, or Sweet and Spicy Peanuts (page 9) for the prepared candied nuts.

# Roquefort Cheese Dressing

**Makes about 2½ cups**

*This dressing has been on the café menu for at least one hundred years. It's so simple and easy to make fresh and from scratch that I never buy bottled dressing. Keeps for one week refrigerated. This is good with wedge lettuce and sliced tomatoes, and as a sauce for chilled, blanched asparagus.*

1½ cups mayonnaise

¾ cup sour cream

¼ cup buttermilk

2 teaspoons Worcestershire sauce

1 teaspoon hot red pepper sauce

1¼ cups crumbled Roquefort cheese

Kosher salt and freshly ground
black pepper

In a 1-quart bowl, whisk together the mayonnaise, sour cream, buttermilk, Worcestershire, and hot red pepper sauce until smooth. Fold in the cheese and season to taste with salt and pepper. Cover and refrigerate for at last 2 hours before using.

**VARIATION**

Substitute reduced-fat mayonnaise and reduced-fat sour cream; however, nonfat does not work with this recipe.

# Champagne Vinaigrette

**Makes 2 cups**

*Champagne vinegar has a bright, aromatic, complex taste. It's made from the same grapes used in Champagne, so it shares some of Champagne's flavors. This is one of my favorite salad dressings. Keeps for two weeks refrigerated. This is good with mixed green salads, and fruit or vegetable salads.*

½ cup Champagne vinegar

2 tablespoons minced shallots

2 tablespoons Dijon mustard

1½ cups extra-virgin olive oil

Kosher salt and freshly ground black or white pepper

In a 1-quart bowl, whisk together the vinegar, shallots, and mustard. Slowly drizzle the olive oil into the bowl, whisking constantly, until all the oil is incorporated and the dressing is thickened. Season to taste with salt and pepper. Cover and let stand for at least 2 hours before using.

## DOUBLE DUTY DRESSINGS

Salad dressing recipes in this chapter can be used not only as dressings for salads but as sauces and spreads. Try the Café Thousand Island Dressing as a spread for panini and as a dipping sauce for crudités. The Roquefort Cheese Dressing makes a good sauce for a platter of blanched vegetables served cold and is a great topping for steamed asparagus. The Champagne Vinaigrette is a good dipping sauce for fruit. The Peanut Butter Dressing is excellent on pasta salads and hot pasta, and as a sauce for grilled chicken and shrimp.

# ❊ Make-Ahead Salads ❊

Everyone likes fresh, crisp salads, but I think they're difficult to make while fixing dinner for the family or entertaining for company. They can take a lot of time to wash, chop, and combine. My solution is to make everything ahead, including the dressing, up to two days in advance. I wash and cut the lettuce, spin it dry, and place it in resealable plastic bags or containers with a clean, dry paper towel in each. Same thing for any chopped or sliced vegetables, including tomatoes, and for fruit, including berries. I grate or chop cheese and refrigerate it, covered. And I make the dressing and refrigerate it separately. When it comes time to serve salad—it's so simple. Put the lettuce in the bowl, add the other ingredients and dressing, toss, and presto! Cold, crisp, fresh—and instant—salad.

# Peanut Butter Dressing

**Makes 2 cups**

*This is yummy not only as a salad dressing for Asian Chicken Salad (page 64), but also to dress pasta salads, and as a dipping sauce for blanched or raw vegetables or grilled chicken strips, and to sauce beef, pork, or chicken satay. Keeps for two weeks refrigerated.*

¾ cup creamy peanut butter

3 tablespoons teriyaki sauce

3 tablespoons lemon juice

3 tablespoons minced fresh cilantro

1 tablespoon sugar

1 teaspoon minced fresh garlic

¼ cup vegetable or peanut oil

1 tablespoon dark sesame oil

¼ cup water

Kosher salt

Hot red pepper sauce

In a 1-quart bowl, whisk together all the ingredients except the oils, water, salt, and hot pepper sauce until smooth. Slowly drizzle in the oils, whisking constantly, until all the oil is incorporated and the dressing is thickened and emulsified. Whisk in the water. Season to taste with salt and hot red pepper sauce. Cover with plastic wrap and let stand for at least 2 hours before using.

# Yesterday's French Dressing

**Makes 2 cups**

*The secret to the flavor of this old-fashioned café dressing is in the water and the sugar. Red wine vinegar can be quite acidic, and I suspect it was even more acidic in the old days. So the water serves to cut the acid and make the taste milder. Add a little sugar and you have a classic old-fashioned French dressing. Keeps for two weeks refrigerated. This is good with mixed greens, fruit, and vegetable salads.*

½ cup red wine vinegar

3 tablespoons water

1 tablespoon lemon juice

1 tablespoon Worcestershire sauce

1 tablespoon Dijon mustard

1 teaspoon sugar

1 teaspoon minced fresh garlic

1 cup vegetable oil

½ cup extra-virgin olive oil

Kosher salt and freshly ground black pepper

In a 1-quart bowl, whisk together all the ingredients except the oils, salt, and pepper until smooth. Slowly drizzle in the oils, whisking constantly, until all the oil is incorporated and the dressing is thickened and emulsified. Season to taste with salt and pepper. Cover with plastic wrap and let stand for at least 2 hours before using.

# Today's French Dressing

**Makes 2 cups**

*Today's French Dressing has my special twist: minced fresh herbs. You may use any combination you like; however, I think basil has the wrong flavor profile. Be sure to mince the herbs fine and use only the leaves, no stems. Keeps for two weeks refrigerated. This is good with mixed greens, fruit, and vegetable salads.*

½ cup red or white wine vinegar or Champagne vinegar

1 tablespoon lemon or lime juice

1 tablespoon Dijon mustard

1 tablespoon minced shallots

1 tablespoon minced fresh garlic

3 tablespoons minced fresh herbs, such as thyme, tarragon, or flat-leaf parsley

¾ cup vegetable oil

¾ cup extra-virgin olive oil

Kosher salt and freshly ground black pepper

In a 1-quart bowl, whisk together the vinegar, lemon juice, mustard, shallots, and garlic until smooth. Stir in the herbs. Slowly drizzle the oils into the bowl, whisking constantly, until all the oil is incorporated and the dressing is thickened and emulsified. Season to taste with salt and pepper. Cover with plastic wrap and let stand for at least 2 hours before using.

# Café Thousand Island Dressing

**Makes 2 cups**

*Thousand Island dressing has been around since 1912. It's a version of the older Russian dressing and the name refers to the small pieces of chopped ingredients that resemble floating islands. It is available in the supermarket in both shelf-stable and refrigerated versions. The refrigerated versions are much more expensive and not nearly as fresh as this homemade version. Keeps for one week refrigerated. This is good with an iceberg lettuce wedge, in Reuben and panini sandwiches, or as a dip for crudités.*

¾ cup light mayonnaise

¼ cup ketchup

¼ cup chile sauce

¼ cup minced green bell pepper

3 tablespoons minced green onion

3 tablespoons minced sweet pickles

1 tablespoon Worcestershire sauce

1 teaspoon hot red pepper sauce

Kosher salt and freshly ground
black pepper

2 hard-boiled eggs, finely chopped

In a 1-quart bowl, mix together all the ingredients except the salt and pepper and the hard-boiled eggs. Season to taste with the salt and pepper. Fold in the chopped eggs.

Cover with plastic wrap and refrigerate for at least 2 hours before using.

## ❊ Ranch in a Jar ❊

The recipe for my children's favorite ranch dressing couldn't be simpler: In a 1-quart mason jar with tight-fitting lid, place 1 cup of light mayo, 1 cup of buttermilk, ½ cup of low-fat sour cream, 1 teaspoon of garlic powder, 1 teaspoon of onion powder, 1 tablespoon of sugar, 1 tablespoon of unseasoned rice vinegar, 1 teaspoon of salt, and 1 tablespoon of dried parsley. Screw on the lid tightly and shake well until all the seasonings are mixed. Makes about 2½ cups. Store in the refrigerator for 2 hours before using. Keeps for 1 week refrigerated.

# CHAPTER 5

# SIDES

# Scene Stealers

My grandmother Carlyn, who was a great cook in most ways, cooked vegetables to death. She boiled cauliflower, Brussels sprouts, spinach, and peas beyond recognition. Carrots were always swimming in a sweet syrupy glaze. Maybe that's why today I like a lot of vegetables raw.

When I went to chef's school at the Culinary Institute of America in Hyde Park, New York, I saw a whole new vegetable world. There were fresh vegetables cooked al dente, new varieties we had never eaten at home, vegetable pâtés, mousses, terrines, soufflés, timbales, court-bouillon with vegetables, and vegetable aspics. It was the 1980s and French cuisine ruled, so I even learned to make sauces just for vegetables. I had never seen such a thing at my grandmother's table, where we all ate Sunday dinner as a family when I was growing up.

Since culinary school, I have learned even more ways of cooking vegetables, for example, steaming, grilling, and baking. But I give my grandmother credit where credit is due. Her mashed potatoes were out of this world. I have taken the traditional texture and flavor that I remember and given them a twist with my recipe for mashed potatoes. I also have two other quick and easy vegetable mashes: Cauliflower Mash and Sweet Potato Mash.

Sides are an important part of any meal; they complete the plate and complement the main protein. And sides are not just vegetables. Consider applesauce. Once you see how simple it is to make homemade applesauce and how terrific it tastes, you'll probably never buy another jar of applesauce again. You can use it as a side, as a sauce for pound cake, gingerbread, or other unfrosted cakes, or in the Walnut-Applesauce Coffee Cake (page 138).

Another nonvegetable side is spaetzle. Berghoff Spaetzle is not like any other spaetzle recipe I have ever tasted because it uses lots of eggs, which accounts for its rich flavor and firm but tender texture. You can make spaetzle plain or with added herbs, and serve them in place of potatoes, noodles, or rice. They also make a great addition to Homemade Chicken Spaetzle Soup (page 29).

Many of the recipes from the café, such as the sides in this chapter, make use of some very basic groceries and ingredients: onions, celery, mushrooms, and potatoes. These basic ingredients are used over and over again in different ways throughout this book. This is no different from the way the Berghoffs cooked at home. Grandma Carlyn was a master at cross-utilizing her food, and that's something I learned not at chef's school but from her.

## A YEAR OF SWEET ONIONS

Onions are so everyday we sometimes take them for granted. Basically, there are two kinds: green and dry. Green, immature onions, sometimes mistakenly called scallions (which are a different, mature vegetable in the same family—green onions have a rounded base; scallions, a straight-sided base), are available year-round. Dry onions are mature onions. Versatile mild-flavored white or yellow onions are available year-round and can be used in almost any recipe. The red onion, also widely available, has a stronger flavor, often welcome for its color and its bite in highly seasoned dishes, such as salsas and salads with citrus. Among dry onions is a very special category: sweet onions, which are good in any dish. If you watch for the different varieties in season, you can purchase sweet onions all year-round. Maui onions, from Hawaii, are sweet and mild and juicy, with a flattened shape, available April to July. Vidalia onions, from Georgia, are large round and pale yellow and available year-round in the South but from May to July elsewhere. Then there is the Walla Walla onion, from Washington State, with a shape and flavor similar to Vidalia's, in season from June to September. Two imported sweet onions are worth looking for in specialty produce markets: Oso, from South America—sweeter than Vidalias—available January through March; and Rio, from South America, available from October to December.

# Applesauce

**Serves 8**

*Applesauce from a jar is good, but it doesn't taste the same as the homemade applesauce I grew up with. My grandmother Carlyn used to quarter but not peel or core the apples, then cook them in a big pot with sugar. After the cooked apples cooled, she would put them in batches through a hand-cranked food mill that separated the skin and seeds from the apple pulp and juice. My applesauce tastes the same as hers, but my recipe takes less than half the time. It can be served warm or cold. And it freezes well in resealable plastic bags for up to one month.*

3 pounds Granny Smith apples, cored, peeled, and cut into eighths

Juice of 1 large lemon

1 cup water

⅓ cup brown sugar

¼ cup granulated sugar

½ teaspoon ground cinnamon

½ teaspoon salt

Place all the ingredients in an 8-quart pot. Cover. Bring to a boil over high heat. Decrease the heat and simmer until the apples are very tender, about 25 minutes.

Remove the pot from the heat. Using a potato masher, mash the apples in the pot to your desired texture: chunky or smooth.

Serve warm, or transfer to a covered dish and refrigerate.

### VARIATION

For a sweeter taste, substitute Golden Delicious apples for the Granny Smiths.

# Berghoff Spaetzle

**Serves 8**

*Berghoff spaetzle are special because we use so many eggs and we cook our spaetzle in chicken broth for additional flavor. The traditional Old World recipe for spaetzle was to use one egg for every person to be served, plus one egg for good measure. Spaetzle dough is pushed through holes in a spaetzle maker into simmering broth below and cooked just until tender. You can also push the dough through a large colander set over the broth. You can mix spaetzle the quick way in a food processor, or the traditional way by mixing by hand in a large bowl. Either way, it's important to let the dough rest for 30 minutes before cooking. You can save any of the leftover cooking broth, refrigerate it, and add it to soups and stews. Spaetzle can also be cooked in water. A cooked spaetzle looks like a tiny, short dumpling about the size of the top joint of your little finger.*

9 large eggs, slightly beaten

1 tablespoon powdered chicken soup base, or 1 chicken bouillon cube, pulverized

⅛ teaspoon baking powder

1 teaspoon kosher salt

¼ teaspoon ground white pepper

3 cups all-purpose flour

3 quarts chicken broth or water

1 tablespoon canola oil

To mix in the food processor: In the work bowl of a food processor fitted with the steel blade, place the eggs, chicken soup base, baking powder, salt, pepper, and flour. Process for 15 seconds. Remove the lid, scrape down the sides with a spatula, replace the lid, and process just until a smooth batter forms, about 15 additional seconds. Transfer the batter to a 1-quart pitcher with a lip. Cover with plastic wrap and let rest for 30 minutes.

To mix in a bowl: In a 3-quart bowl, combine the eggs, chicken soup base, baking powder, salt, pepper, and 1 cup of the flour. Stir or whisk until the flour is absorbed and the batter is smooth. Add the second cup of flour in small batches and stir or whisk until the batter is smooth and thick. Repeat with the third cup of flour. Transfer to a 1-quart pitcher with a lip. Cover with plastic wrap and let rest for 30 minutes.

To cook: In an 8-quart pot, bring the chicken broth to a boil. Place the spaetzle maker or a metal colander with ¼-inch holes over the briskly simmering broth. Add the spaetzle dough in three batches, about 1 cup each. If using a colander, push the dough through the holes with a rubber spatula. Cook each batch, stirring gently with a rubber spatula, until the spaetzle rise to the top, 3 to 4 minutes. Remove them using a large slotted spoon or long-handled perforated metal skimmer, and transfer to a large colander set on a dinner plate. Transfer the cooked spaetzle to a bowl of ice-cold water. Repeat until all the spaetzle dough is used. After the last batch has cooled in the cold water (about 2 minutes), drain the spaetzle well. Place the spaetzle in a bowl and toss with the canola oil. You can refrigerate the spaetzle, covered with plastic wrap, for up to 3 days.

To add to soups and stews: Stir in the cooked spaetzle right before serving and cook just to heat through.

To serve as a side dish: Heat 2 tablespoons of butter in a large skillet and sauté the spaetzle, in batches, until heated through and slightly browned, adding more butter as necessary. Serve immediately.

### VARIATION

For herbed spaetzle, stir 3 tablespoons (total) of minced fresh herbs into the batter. One tablespoon each of flat-leaf parsley, thyme, and dill is a nice combination.

# ❈ Spaetzle ❈

These tiny dumplings are a specialty in Germany and certain regions of Austria (*knopfle* or *knodel*), Switzerland (*knopfli*), Hungary (*nokedli*), and France (*spätzle*). The word *spätzle* in German means "little sparrow." Although the dough can be made firm enough to cut on a board like noodles, the most traditional dough is soft enough to be forced through the holes of a spaetzle maker. The dumplings are cooked by dropping them into a large pot of boiling broth or water. Several kinds of inexpensive spaetzle makers are available. The one I use is a slide spaetzle maker. About 13 inches long and 4½ inches wide, it is flat, chromed metal, with approximately ¼-inch holes in its surface and a small dough hopper that slides back and forth over the perforated surface.

# Green Beans

**Serves 8**

*Green beans are available year-round; however, the peak season is May to October. In my grandmother's day, green beans were called string beans because of the long fibrous "string" that ran down the length of the bean. Today, these strings have been mostly bred out of the bean, so there's no need to destring them. Just cut off the stem, rinse, and you're ready to cook a highly flavored vegetable side dish that goes with meat, poultry, or fish.*

6 slices thick, smoked pepper bacon

3 tablespoons butter

4 quarts water

3 pounds green beans, trimmed

Kosher salt and cracked black pepper

Cook the bacon in a 12-inch skillet over medium-high heat, until crisp. Remove the bacon from the pan and lay on paper towels to drain excess fat. Crumble the bacon and set aside.

Discard all but 1 tablespoon of the bacon fat in the pan. Add the butter over low heat to melt. Remove the pan from the heat.

Bring the water to a boil in an 8-quart pot. Add the beans and cook until crisp-tender, about 3 minutes. Remove the beans and drain.

Return the skillet with the bacon fat and butter to medium heat. Add the beans and toss to coat well and heat through. Stir in the crumbled bacon and season to taste with salt and pepper. Serve hot.

## VARIATIONS

The beans can be blanched in advance, chilled in an ice water bath to stop the cooking, drained, then heated to order.

Substitute turkey bacon for the pepper bacon.

For a vegetarian dish, omit the bacon, decrease the butter to 2 tablespoons, and sauté with ¼ to ½ cup slivered almonds, chopped pecans or chopped cashews.

# Navy Beans and Bacon

**Serves 8**

*Navy beans are white, pea-size beans with a mild flavor and a smooth texture. They earned their nickname because they were a staple in the United States Navy diet during the late nineteenth and early twentieth centuries. They come both dried and canned. The great thing about canned beans in general is that there is not much difference in the nutritional value between them and those cooked from scratch.*

1 pound bacon

2 tablespoons reserved bacon fat

1 cup chopped yellow onion

1 cup chopped celery

1 teaspoon chopped fresh garlic

1½ cups chicken broth

4 (15-ounce) cans small white or great Northern beans, drained and rinsed (see Note)

Freshly ground black pepper

In an 8-quart pot, sauté the bacon over medium heat until crispy. Remove the bacon from the pot and drain all but 2 tablespoons of fat. Coarsely chop the bacon and set aside. In the same pot, heat the reserved bacon fat over medium heat. Add the onion, celery, and garlic, and sauté until translucent but not browned, about 5 minutes. Do not drain. Add the broth, beans, and bacon, and simmer for about 10 minutes over medium heat. Season to taste with pepper.

*Note:* To prepare this recipe using dried beans: Rinse and drain 1 pound of dried navy beans. Remove and discard any stones. Place the beans in an 8-quart pot and cover with 2 quarts of water. Bring to a boil over medium-high heat. Remove from the heat and let sit, covered, for 1 hour. Drain and set the beans aside. In the same pot, proceed with the recipe from the beginning. Add the partially cooked beans, reserved bacon, and 1 quart (instead of 1½ cups) chicken broth. Simmer, covered, until the beans are tender but not falling apart, 1½ to 2 hours.

# Lyonnaise Potatoes

**Serves 8 to 10**

*Potatoes, onions, and parsley—such a simple recipe, but once again it shows how some basic ingredients can be reused, recycled, and reinvented. The dish originated in Lyon, France, and there are dozens of versions, some with precooked, some with raw potatoes. My twist is to toss the sliced potatoes and onions in olive oil before cooking, so the vegetables are evenly coated and the finished dish is not swimming in fat. If you have a mandoline, use it to slice the potatoes and onions evenly. Slice the potatoes diagonally and lengthwise for nice long slices. This is a great big potato cake, so slice it into wedges and plate it in the kitchen. I slide the potato cake out on a twelve-inch pizza pan for slicing.*

3 medium to large yellow onions, sliced ⅛ inch thick

4 tablespoons extra-virgin olive oil

2 teaspoons kosher salt

1 teaspoon ground white pepper

1½ pounds unpeeled russet or Yukon Gold potatoes, sliced diagonally, lengthwise ⅛ inch thick

¼ cup chopped fresh flat-leaf parsley

Preheat the oven to 400°F.

In a 3-quart bowl, place the onions, 2 tablespoons of the oil, 1 teaspoon of the salt, and ½ teaspoon of the pepper. Toss well to coat and set aside.

In another 3-quart bowl, place the potatoes and the remaining 2 tablespoons of oil, salt, and pepper. Toss well to coat and set aside.

Spray a 12-inch nonstick ovenproof sauté pan lightly with nonstick cooking spray and heat over medium-high heat. Add the onions and sauté, stirring, until golden brown but not burned, about 15 minutes. Transfer the onions to a large plate and set aside.

Spray the same sauté pan lightly with nonstick cooking spray, and, over lower heat, layer half of the potato slices in an overlapping spiral to cover the bottom of the skillet (see page 92). Spread the reserved onions evenly over the potatoes. Top with the remaining potato slices, in an overlapping spiral. Press down evenly with a spatula.

Place the sauté pan in the preheated oven and bake, uncovered, until the potatoes are cooked through and the top is golden, 35 to 40 minutes.

Remove the pan from the oven. Let sit for 5 minutes. Carefully loosen the edges and bottom of the potatoes with a nonstick spatula. Slide the potato cake onto a large cutting board or pizza pan for slicing. Sprinkle with fresh parsley, slice into eight or ten wedges, and serve immediately with meat, poultry, or fish. Or, for a vegetarian entrée, serve with an omelet.

# Peas and Carrots

**Serves 8**

*When I was growing up, baby carrots didn't exist, but peas and carrots were a familiar combination in most restaurants, including the Berghoff Café. Yes, you can buy them in a can and you can buy them frozen. But I have updated our old-fashioned recipe and combine real carrots with convenient frozen peas in winter and fresh peas in spring. The cooking broth serves as the sauce.*

1 tablespoon unsalted butter

1 cup sliced yellow onion

3 cups peeled, diagonally sliced fresh carrots, preferably organic

½ teaspoon salt

1 cup vegetable broth, preferably organic

2 cups frozen green peas

In a 3-quart saucepan over medium heat, melt the butter. Add the onion and sauté, stirring, until translucent but not brown, about 3 minutes. Add the carrots, salt, and broth. Cover and bring to a boil over high heat. Decrease the heat and simmer, covered, until just tender, about 15 minutes.

Remove the lid and add the peas. Stir and cook until just tender, about 3 minutes.

Transfer to a serving bowl and serve some of the broth with each serving.

### VARIATION
In spring when fresh peas are in season, substitute fresh peas for frozen. Cook until just tender, about 5 minutes.

# Cauliflower Mash

**Serves 8**

*This is quick, easy, and very versatile. It can be served as a side dish for meat, poultry, or fish, and I like to use it as a bed for sliced roast ham or pork.*

2 heads cauliflower

1 teaspoon salt

1 bay leaf

4 ounces low-fat sour cream

2 tablespoons chopped fresh parsley

2 teaspoons freshly ground black pepper

Pinch of salt

Trim the cauliflower, discarding the leaves. Cut the cauliflower into 1-inch chunks. Place the cauliflower, salt, and bay leaf in an 8-quart pot, and add enough water to cover by 1 inch. Bring to a boil, lower to a simmer, and cook until very tender, about 20 minutes. Drain the cauliflower and discard the bay leaf. Return the cauliflower to the pot and mash well with a potato masher. For a smoother purée, use a handheld immersion blender after you have mashed the cauliflower.

Place the pot over low heat and add the sour cream and parsley. Season with the pepper and salt. Stir well to mix. Serve immediately.

# Sautéed Mushrooms Jus Lié

**Serves 8**

*Mushrooms Jus Lié has been part of the Berghoff menu for 100 years. On the 1932 menu, it was listed simply as "Mushroom Sauce" and went with two Berghoff plates: Braised Sweetbreads on Toast with Mushroom Sauce, sixty cents, and Broiled Beef Tenderloin Steak, Sliced Tomatoes and Mushroom Sauce, eighty cents. We suspect it became Mushrooms Jus Lié in 1948 starting with the sixteen-year rule of our classically trained European chef Karl Hertenstein. Call it sauce or jus lié (French for lightly thickened meat juice), something wonderful happens to plain white mushrooms when they are sautéed and braised in a little beef broth. This makes a tasty sauce for almost any meat, chicken, and even omelets.*

1 tablespoon unsalted butter

1 teaspoon minced fresh garlic

1 pound white button mushrooms, sliced

2 cups prepared beef broth

Kosher salt and freshly ground black pepper

1 tablespoon cornstarch

2 tablespoons water

¼ cup minced fresh parsley

In a 12-inch skillet over medium-high heat, melt the butter. Add the garlic and sauté for 2 minutes. Add the mushrooms and sauté, stirring, until golden brown, 5 to 6 minutes. Pour in the broth and bring to a boil. Decrease the heat and simmer until the liquid is reduced by half, about 8 minutes. Season to taste with salt and pepper.

Mix the cornstarch with the water to form a smooth paste. Whisk the cornstarch paste into the mushroom mixture and simmer, stirring, until the sauce thickens and the cornstarch is cooked and clear, about 4 minutes. Sprinkle in the parsley. Remove from the heat and keep warm until ready to use.

# Asparagus Vinaigrette

**Serves 8**

*This makes a great side dish in spring and summer, and a great buffet dish in fall. The asparagus is trimmed, cut into 2-inch lengths—which makes it look like there are lots of asparagus tips—and it is easy to blanch, drain, and chill. The vinaigrette is drizzled on right before serving. Depending on my mood and the other courses that it will accompany, I use Champagne Vinaigrette (page 73), Yesterday's French Dressing (page 76), Today's French Dressing (page 77), Ranch Dressing (page 79), or—really indulgent—Roquefort Cheese Dressing (page 72).*

3 pounds fresh asparagus, ends trimmed

1 teaspoon kosher salt

4 quarts water

1 cup Berghoff salad dressing of choice (see above)

Wash and trim the asparagus of any woody ends. Starting with the tip end, cut on the bias into 2-inch lengths.

Cook the asparagus in boiling, lightly salted water for 3 minutes. Drain in a colander and rinse well under cold running water to stop the cooking and set the color. When the asparagus has cooled to room temperature, drain well. Spread on several thicknesses of paper towels and pat dry. Cover and refrigerate until ready to serve.

To serve: Arrange the asparagus on a serving platter. Drizzle with your dressing of choice. Serve immediately.

## VEGETABLES VINAIGRETTE

When I was first married, we entertained for dinner a lot and several of my friends marveled that whatever vegetable I served vinaigrette style was bright, crisp, and colorful, not limp and yellowed. I knew that if you let vegetables, particularly green ones, stand for long in a dressing that contains acid—vinegar or lemon juice—it will dull their color and diminish their texture. So I always blanch my vegetables in advance and chill them, then add the dressing right before serving.

# Sweet Potato Mash

**Serves 8**

*In our family, this replaces the traditional Thanksgiving sweet potato–marshmallow casserole. And it's so easy to make that I serve it not just on holidays but all year long.*

3 pounds sweet potatoes,
peeled and cut into eighths

1 quart chicken or vegetable broth

1 teaspoon salt

¼ cup brown sugar

1 tablespoon butter

Pinch of ground cinnamon

Place the potatoes, broth, and salt into an 8-quart pot over medium heat and cover. Bring to a boil. Decrease the heat and simmer, covered, until the potatoes are very tender, about 20 minutes.

Drain the potatoes, reserving all of the liquid. Return the potatoes to the pot and, using a potato masher, mash well. Add 1 to 1½ cups of the reserved cooking liquid and the sugar, and whip with the potato masher until smooth. Add the butter and whip until melted.

Serve warm, with a pinch of cinnamon.

## REVIVING COLD POTATOES

A *cold potato* in colloquial English means a worthless person—that's how poorly we feel about leftover refrigerated potatoes. But it's a shame to throw away good mashed potatoes, so here's a way to reheat them: Place the cold mashed potatoes in a lidded double boiler. (If you don't have one, put them in a small pot just big enough to hold them. Cover with a lid. Place that pot in a larger pot with water 2 inches deep.) Heat over low heat until the potatoes are hot and fluffy. Whisk and serve—good as new. You can also re-heat Lyonnaise Potatoes (page 91) by wrapping the leftover portion in aluminum foil that has been lightly sprayed with nonstick cooking spray. Place the foil-wrapped potatoes on a pizza pan and warm in a preheated 350°F oven until hot, about 20 minutes. Garnish with chopped fresh parsley.

# Mashed Potatoes

**Serves 8**

*Everybody loves mashed potatoes, especially the way our family always made them. Peel and boil the potatoes, put them through a ricer so they are not lumpy, then whip them up with lots of milk and/or cream and butter. My twist is quick, easy, just as tasty, and has only a fraction of the fat. Any unused cooking liquid can be saved, refrigerated, and added to soups and stews.*

**3 pounds russet or all-purpose white potatoes, peeled and cut into eighths**

**1 quart chicken or vegetable broth, preferably organic**

**1 teaspoon salt**

**2 tablespoons unsalted butter**

**Freshly ground black pepper (optional)**

In an 8-quart pot, place the potatoes, broth, and salt. Cover and bring to a boil. Decrease the heat and simmer until the potatoes are very tender, about 20 minutes.

Drain the potatoes, reserving all of the liquid. Return the potatoes to the pot and, using a potato masher, mash well. Add 1 to 1½ cups of the reserved cooking liquid and whip with the potato masher until smooth. Add the butter and whip until melted.

Serve warm, with pepper if desired.

**VARIATION**
Substitute Yukon Gold potatoes for russet or white.

# TODAYS SPECIALS

**CORNED BEEF HASH**
SERVED W/ 2 EGGS & TOAST
5 50

**BBQ CHICKEN SALAD**
SERVED W/ RANCH DRESSING
6 25

**HOMEMADE CHILI OVER BERGHOFF CHIPS**
SERVED W/ SOUR CREAM & CHEDDAR CHEESE
6 25

**SLOPPY JOE**
W/ BERGHOFF CHIPS
6 75

**CHIPOTLE CHICK**
W/ BERGHOFF
6 25

GREEK SALAD

# CHAPTER 6

## BERGHOFF PLATES

# Daily Specials

Like many diners and restaurants in the country, especially during and right after the Great Depression, the Berghoff Café featured the popular "plate" lunches and dinners. These were a complete meal on a plate—protein, starch, and a vegetable—good food and lots of it at a good price. But what customers

perhaps didn't know was that it was also a good deal for the restaurant. Restaurants buy in quantity—tuna fish comes in 48-can cases, cheese in 40-pound blocks or wheels, potatoes in 50-pound sacks, flour in 50-pound bags. A restaurant always has a lot of ingredients, and what better way to use up the excess than by creating a daily special.

Daily specials were straightforward and easy to cook, tasted great, and they were a terrific value for the money. We still think they are all of the above and we still have them at the café today. I list them at "Carlyn's Ceiling Prices," named after a 1945 menu that my grandfather Lewis W. Berghoff filed with the War Price and Rationing Board, listing "Our

Ceiling Prices," which were unlawful to change in any way. The daily specials are always sellouts.

Even though the daily special plate lunches and dinners started in restaurants, there is every reason to serve them at home. They are simple, easy recipes and your menu is made for you. The dishes have wide appeal and you can cook most in advance. Even the schnitzels are breaded and refrigerated and ready for last-minute frying. And what could be easier than serving complete plates from kitchen to table?

The following are some of my favorite plate dinners from the café and from my home, created from recipes throughout this book:

## BERGHOFF PLATE DINNERS

In 1932, the Berghoff featured "plate dinners," served from 11 a.m. to 11 p.m. For thirty-five cents, customers could choose between Fresh Thuringer Sausage with Boiled Potatoes and Sauerkraut; English Beef Stew, with Spring Vegetables and Mashed Potatoes; Roast Loin of Pork, with Applesauce; Roast Stuffed Breast of Veal, with Carrots and Peas; and—a tradition not ready for revival—Homemade Head Cheese with Potato Salad.

- Meat Balls with Red Sauce (page 104) served over spaghetti or as an entrée

- Classic Salisbury Steak with Asparagus Vinaigrette, Spaetzle, and Mushrooms Jus Lié (page 107)

- Carlyn's Stew du Jour with Vegetables (page 103)

- Beer-Braised Pork Loin with Applesauce and Asparagus Vinaigrette (page 114)

- Bourbon-Basted Baked Ham with Navy Beans and Bacon and Sweet Potato Mash (page 112)

- Turkey Meat Loaf with Green Beans and Lyonnaise Potatoes (page 110)

- Schnitzels with Mashed Potatoes and Peas and Carrots (page 108)

But please feel free to mix and match the recipes in this book to make your own unique special plates.

# Carlyn's Stew du Jour with Vegetables

**Serves 8 to 10**

*There are many features I like about this stew. First, I can cook it one or two days ahead and refrigerate it, then reheat it the day I want to serve it, and the flavors are even better. Second, I can use any kind of cubed meat or poultry that I'm in the mood for. Third, I use vegetables that are available year round; and last, it makes a great family dinner or buffet dish.*

3 tablespoons vegetable oil

3 pounds skinless boneless meat or poultry (beef, veal, pork, lamb, chicken breast or thigh, turkey breast or thigh), cut into 1-inch cubes

⅓ cup all-purpose flour

½ teaspoon kosher salt

½ teaspoon freshly ground black pepper

2 cups sliced yellow onion

2 teaspoons chopped fresh garlic

½ cup tomato paste

2 bay leaves

4 cups broth (beef for beef, veal, lamb, or pork; chicken for chicken or turkey; vegetable for all)

1 cup white wine

2 cups red-skinned potatoes, cut into ½-inch cubes

1 cup halved baby carrots

4 cups sliced mushrooms

Heat the oil in a Dutch oven over medium-high heat. In a bowl, toss the meat or poultry cubes with the flour, salt, and pepper, and cook in batches in the hot oil, stirring gently until browned, 3 to 4 minutes. Do not overcrowd the pan. As the meat is browned, transfer to a large tray. Add more oil by the tablespoon to the Dutch oven, if necessary.

Add the onion and garlic to the same Dutch oven and cook, over medium-high heat, 5 minutes, stirring occasionally. Return the meat to the pot, stir in the tomato paste and bay leaves, and continue to cook for 5 minutes, stirring occasionally. Add the broth and wine, decrease the heat and simmer until the meat is almost tender, stirring occasionally, about 1½ hours for beef, pork, or veal, 45 minutes for chicken or turkey. Add the potatoes and carrots, and cook for another 30 minutes. Remove the bay leaves and discard. Add the mushrooms and cook for another 10 minutes. Adjust the seasonings. Serve warm with noodles, rice, or mashed root vegetables.

The stew may be made and refrigerated, up to 4 days ahead, or frozen up to 2 weeks. Reheat gently in a 350°F oven, or on the stovetop in a hot water bath or using a heat diffuser.

# Meatballs with Red Sauce

**Serves 8 to 10/Makes 32 meatballs**

*When I make these meatballs I use whatever ground meat that strikes my fancy (especially when there is a special at my local market). I can serve them over cooked spaghetti with grated Parmesan. Or else I can serve them in their sauce with a side of green beans and cooked egg noodles. They also make a wonderful buffet dish and great appetizer meatballs.*

## MEATBALLS

3 tablespoons unsalted butter

1 cup minced onion

3 pounds lean ground meat or
a mixture of any combination of
veal, pork, lamb, and/or beef

1 cup fresh white bread crumbs (page 57)

3 large eggs, beaten

½ cup milk

2 teaspoons kosher salt

2 teaspoons freshly ground black pepper

½ teaspoon ground nutmeg

Vegetable or olive oil, for frying

2 quarts Red Sauce (page 105)

Heat 2 tablespoons of the butter in a Dutch oven over medium-high heat; add the onion and sauté until lightly browned, about 6 minutes. Remove from the heat; let cool.

In large bowl, mix the meat(s), bread crumbs, eggs, milk, salt, pepper, nutmeg, and sautéed onion until well blended. Form the mixture into thirty-two meatballs (a scant 3 tablespoons each). Place on a baking sheet, cover, and refrigerate for at least 1 to 2 hours, until firm.

Heat the oil in a 12-inch sauté pan over medium-high heat; add eight meatballs to the sauté pan and brown on all sides, turning frequently. Remove the browned meatballs and drain on paper towels while repeating three times using more batches of meatballs. Set aside.

In the same Dutch oven used for browning the onion, add the Red Sauce and bring to a simmer. Add the browned meatballs to the Dutch oven with the sauce and stir to mix well. Return to a simmer and cook for 20 minutes, until the meatballs are heated through completely. Keep warm until ready to serve.

Serve over 2 pounds of cooked spaghetti with grated Parmesan cheese and accompany with garlic bread and a green salad.

Or serve with Green Beans (page 88) and Mashed Potatoes (page 99); or with Cauliflower Mash (page 94) and Iceberg Wedge with Roquefort Dressing and Bacon (page 61).

**VARIATION**

The meatballs can be sprayed with nonstick cooking spray and baked on a baking sheet in a 375°F oven for 20 to 25 minutes, instead of frying as directed above.

# Red Sauce

**Makes 1 quart**

*This recipe can easily be doubled, using a 6-quart saucepan.*

2 tablespoons olive oil

½ cup finely diced onion

1 tablespoon chopped fresh garlic

1 (28-ounce) can crushed tomatoes

1 (10¾-ounce can) tomato purée (about 1 cup)

1½ cups chicken broth

1 tablespoon chopped fresh basil

2 teaspoons chopped fresh oregano

1 tablespoon sugar

¼ teaspoon red pepper flakes

Salt and freshly ground black pepper

Heat the oil in a 3-quart saucepan until hot; add the onion and sauté for 1 to 2 minutes. Add the garlic and sauté for 1 minute. Add the crushed tomatoes, tomato purée, broth, 2 teaspoons of the fresh basil, 1 teaspoon of the fresh oregano, and the sugar and pepper flakes; bring to a boil, lower the heat to a simmer, and cook for 50 to 60 minutes, stirring occasionally. Adjust the seasoning with salt and pepper and stir in the remaining teaspoon of both the basil and oregano. Remove from the heat and keep warm.

# Classic Salisbury Steak with Mushroom Jus Lié and Spaetzle

**Serves 8**

*Salisbury steak is minced or ground beef shaped to look like a steak and traditionally served with a brown sauce. It was invented by Dr. James H. Salisbury (1823–1905), an American physician, who believed that our teeth are "meat teeth" and our digestive systems are designed for meat. He recommended a daily diet of two-thirds meat and one-third fruit, vegetables, and starch. And he prescribed eating Salisbury steak three times a day.*

*Salisbury steak is a big hit at the café, but so far nobody orders it three times a day.*

5 pounds ground round steak

2 teaspoons kosher salt

1 teaspoon ground black pepper

4 tablespoons fat or vegetable oil

Asparagus Vinaigrette (page 96)

Spaetzle (page 85)

Sautéed Mushrooms Jus Lié (page 95)

In 4-quart bowl, combine the meat, salt, and pepper; stir to mix. Divide the meat into eight portions and, dipping your hands into a bowl of ice water to keep the meat from sticking, shape each portion into oval patties about ¾ inch thick. Heat the fat in a skillet and panfry the patties, or broil for 4 to 6 minutes per side until cooked through. Remove the patties and keep warm.

## TEN, TWO, AND SIX O'CLOCK— HOW TO ARRANGE A PLATE LUNCH ON THE PLATE

If I close my eyes. I still can see the plates we use to serve plate lunches on at the restaurant. They were divided into three sections: one for the vegetables, one for the starch, and one for the protein. So if you look at a dinner plate as a clock, imagine that your vegetables are at ten o'clock, your potatoes or starch at two o'clock, and your fish, poultry, or meat at six o'clock. When it comes to something like stew or spaghetti, of course, the theory breaks down. But I still like to put some grated cheese at ten o'clock, some fresh chopped parsley at two o'clock, and the meatballs at six. Beef or meat stew? Chopped chives or parsley at ten, a spoonful of sour cream at two, and crisp, crumbled bacon at six.

Serve with Asparagus Vinaigrette (page 96), Spaetzle, and Sautéed Mushrooms Jus Lié.

# ❉ Schnitzels ❉

**Serves 8**

*Wiener schnitzels, or veal cutlets, were and are one of the best-loved dishes at the Berghoff restaurant. In the café and at home, we make schnitzels from less pricey chicken, turkey, or pork cutlets. For chicken cutlets, I use skinless, boneless breast; for turkey, slices of skinless, boneless breast or thigh: for pork, sliced pork tenderloin.*

2 cups all-purpose flour

1 teaspoon kosher salt

1 teaspoon ground black pepper

5 large eggs, lightly beaten

¼ cup water or milk

½ teaspoon hot red pepper sauce

3 to 6 cups cracker meal or fine dry bread crumbs (see Note)

2½ pounds chicken, turkey, or pork cutlets

Vegetable oil, as needed, for panfrying

Lemon wedges, for garnish

In a medium-size bowl, blend the flour, salt, and pepper. In another medium-size bowl, whisk together the eggs, water, and hot sauce until blended. In a third medium-size bowl, place half of the bread crumbs.

The meat may be in portions of 2 to 5 ounces each. Using a rolling pin or meat mallet, pound the meat cutlets between plastic wrap until evenly thin. Set up a breading station with the seasoned flour, the egg mixture, and then the bread crumbs all in a row. At the end of the line, set a parchment paper–lined baking sheet. Entirely coat each cutlet with the flour mixture and shake off the excess flour before dipping into the egg mixture to coat completely. Shake off the excess egg mixture before coating totally in the crumb mixture. When all the crumbs are used, add the remaining crumbs to the bowl. Lay the cutlets in an even, flat layer on the baking sheet. When all the meat is coated and laid on the baking sheet, cover with plastic wrap and chill for 30 minutes before cooking.

To cook: Pour the oil to a depth of ¼ inch in a large, heavy skillet and heat over medium-high heat. When hot, gently slide the breaded cutlets into the oil, in batches, making sure the cutlets are not touching one another. Do not overcrowd the pan. Cook until lightly browned on one side, 2 to 3 minutes. Turn once with tongs and cook until browned and crisp. Remove from the skillet and drain on paper towel–lined baking sheets. Keep warm in a 200°F oven, uncovered, until ready to serve (see Note). Divide the cutlets into eight portions and serve with lemon wedges.

## VARIATION

Accompany the Schnitzels with Red Sauce (page 105) or Sautéed Mushrooms Jus Lié (page 95).

*Note:* Schnitzels may be breaded and browned up to three days in advance. Keep covered and refrigerated. Reheat on a baking sheet in a 350°F oven for 20 minutes, or until just heated through. Schnitzels will dry out if overheated.

To make your own cracker crumbs, process unsalted crackers in the food processor until fine crumbs form.

# SARAH'S VEGETARIAN BLUE PLATE SPECIALS

At age eleven, my daughter Sarah announced she was a vegetarian—cold turkey, just like that.

I replied that she could be a lacto-ovo vegetarian (for the sake of protein), but if she wanted to be a vegan she would have to wait until she was grown up and do that on her own time. Because Sarah naturally loves animals, I understood where she was coming from, and it has been fairly easy to feed her well. For example, I pulled together the following vegetarian Blue Plate Specials for her, each with a protein:

- Cauliflower Mash, Green Beans, and Stuffed Celery with Pimiento Cheese
- Sweet Potato Mash, Asparagus Vinaigrette, and Swiss Cheese Panini (without sausage)
- Homemade Applesauce, Peas and Carrots, and All-Day, All-Night Egg Sandwich (without bacon)

# Turkey Meat Loaf

**Serves 8**

*Our tasty café meat loaf is made from turkey, and my family and I like it so much I often cook it at home. The barbecue sauce is the perfect seasoning and everybody has a favorite brand, so use yours. The vegetables keep it moist and juicy. I mince the vegetables so the texture of the cooked meat loaf is smooth and dense and it doesn't fall apart when sliced.*

2 pounds ground turkey

2 large eggs

⅓ cup barbecue sauce

½ cup finely chopped green, red, yellow, or orange bell pepper

½ cup finely chopped sweet onion

½ cup finely chopped fresh button mushrooms

½ teaspoon kosher salt

½ teaspoon freshly ground black pepper

¼ to ½ cup dry bread crumbs, as needed

Preheat the oven to 350°F.

In a large bowl, combine the meat, eggs, and barbecue sauce, and mix well with a wooden spoon or rubber spatula. Stir in the pepper, onion, mushrooms, salt, and pepper, and mix gently. Slowly add the bread crumbs and mix just to thicken the loaf. The mixture should be moist and thick, but not firm and dry.

Line an 11 by 4-inch baking pan or a 9 by 5-inch loaf pan with aluminum foil and spray with nonstick cooking spray. Place the meat mixture in the pan and smooth out the top.

Bake until cooked through but not dried out, about 50 minutes. Remove from the heat and let stand for 10 minutes before slicing to serve.

Serve with Green Beans (page 88) and Lyonnaise Potatoes (page 91). Leftover meat loaf makes great sandwiches the next day on a French roll with extra barbecue sauce.

# Bourbon-Basted Baked Ham

**Serves 8**

*I have always loved ham but hated that so many recipes coated it with a sweet, sticky, heavy sauce before roasting it. I love the combination of bourbon and ham. So I developed a recipe for a not-too-sweet way to combine the two.*

1 (7- to 8-pound) fully cooked, bone-in, shank or butt portion, half ham

2 cups water

½ cup Berghoff Bourbon

½ cup apple juice

¼ cup Dusseldorf or brown mustard

1 teaspoon ground white pepper

Preheat the oven to 325°F.

Trim any skin and excess fat from the ham down to a ¼-inch layer of surface fat. Using a sharp knife, cut the fat diagonally in a diamond pattern.

Place the ham on a rack in a roasting pan with 3- to 4-inch-deep sides. Pour the water into the bottom.

In a small bowl, whisk together the bourbon, apple juice, mustard, and pepper. Brush ¼ cup of the bourbon mixture over the surface of the ham.

Bake for 30 minutes. Remove from the oven and brush the ham with another ¼ cup of the bourbon mixture. Bake for another 30 minutes. Repeat until all the bourbon mixture has been used and the ham has baked for 2 hours (and the internal temperature is 140°F as measured by an instant-read meat thermometer). During the last 30 minutes and the bastings, you can also brush with any accumulated pan juices.

Remove from the oven and transfer the ham to a serving platter. Cover loosely with foil and let rest for 15 to 20 minutes. Carve into ⅛-inch-thick slices and serve with Navy Beans and Bacon (page 89) and Sweet Potato Mash (page 98).

# ⚸ The Blue Plate Special ⚸

Blue plate special—the term and the meal—is an American invention. Food historians squabble about its origins. The divided plates were manufactured during the Depression and one model was, indeed, blue; another was the familiar Blue Willow pattern. The term apparently became common in the 1920s when diners and other restaurants started advertising their "blue plate specials," which were complete meals at good prices, served on one plate. One thing all blue plate specials had in common: no substitutions!

# Beer-Braised Pork Loin

**Serves 8 to 10**

*I grew up eating pork roast more often than chicken, which, for many years, was more expensive than meat in my family's restaurants. That's because until the 1950s, chickens were raised on family farms and valued for their eggs. Modern poultry mass-production changed all that. And today's pork is a lot leaner than the pork of my childhood. This roast has the flavors of our family dinners at Grandmother Carlyn's house, but just a fraction of the fat. Some love fennel seeds, some don't, so I made it optional.*

1 (4½- to 5-pound) pork loin roast

1 tablespoon kosher salt

2 teaspoons cracked black pepper

3 tablespoons vegetable oil

2 cups sliced onion

1 tablespoon minced fresh garlic

3 Granny Smith apples, peeled, cored, and sliced ¼ inch thick

1 (12-ounce) bottle Berghoff Original Lager

1 tablespoon fennel seeds, toasted and crushed (optional)

Season the pork liberally with salt and pepper.

Heat 2 tablespoons of the oil in a Dutch oven with a lid over medium-high heat; sear the pork, turning it, until browned on all sides, about 8 minutes. Remove the roast, place on a plate, and set aside.

Remove the excess fat from the Dutch oven and add the remaining tablespoon of oil. Add the onion and sauté until tender, about 3 minutes. Stir in the garlic and cook for 1 minute. Add the apples and cook until they are golden brown, about 5 minutes. Deglaze the pan by adding the Berghoff beer; bring the beer to a boil and add the fennel seeds if desired. Return the seared pork loin to the Dutch oven and bring the liquid to a simmer. Cover the pot, decrease the heat to low, and simmer until fork tender, 2 to 2½ hours. Remove from the heat. Place the roast on a plate, loosely covered with foil. Pour the pan sauce into a 1-quart glass measuring pitcher and skim the excess fat off the top. Purée if desired. Transfer the sauce to a 1-quart saucepan and heat to a simmer.

Serve the pork sliced, with Applesauce (page 83) and Asparagus Vinaigrette (page 96). You can also cut into chunks or shred it over cooked noodles with the pan sauce. You can slice leftover pork and serve it as a sandwich on rye bread with mustard, accompanied by coleslaw.

## HEAT DIFFUSERS

The gas and electric stoves we take for granted today were not household fixtures until the 1930s. The first gas stove (patented in 1826) was shown at the 1851 World's Fair in London, England, and the first electric stove (developed in the 1880s) was shown in 1893 at Chicago's Columbian Exposition, where Herman Berghoff was selling his beer. The spread of both electric and gas stoves depended on cities and towns being electrified and the growth of the gas pipeline network. However, modulating the heat on the earliest stoves was neither quick nor easy, and heat diffusers became popular. Also known as "flame tamers," "pot watchers," or "simmer rings," a heat diffuser is a stovetop utensil that evenly distributes the heat from the stove across the pan or pot bottom. They are usually round disks (some with handles) and can be made of perforated metal, enameled cast iron, or even copper. Different models of heat diffusers can be used on gas or electric stoves and are useful even today for simmering or slowly reheating dishes.

# CHAPTER 7

## CAFÉ PIZZAS

# A New Tradition

Back in 1898 when the café first opened, there were no pizzas—except in Italy. Of course, pizzas were being made by first-generation Italians in their homes, and, beginning in the early 1900s, a handful of pizza restaurants opened on the East Coast. But in the 1950s, after American soldiers

returned from World War II duty in Europe, they brought a taste for pizzas with them, and pizzerias became mainstream.

Pizzas didn't come to the Berghoff Café until 1998, when we opened the café at O'Hare airport in Chicago. They were wildly popular with travelers. Because people equate familiar food with comfort, we use tomato sauce on

the pizzas at the café at the airport. But when we remodeled the café in Chicago-proper, located downstairs from the main restaurant, we added pizzas there. Now pizzas are a year-round menu item at the Berghoff Café but, as is our way, we have created some strictly Berghoff varieties. From these we have chosen five of our favorites, all made with our homemade dough, which are easy to cook at home. You will notice that we do not use red sauce on these Berghoff pizzas. Instead, we add other flavors such as a caraway-seed crust, brown mustard sauce, and an herb crust. Once you cook and taste one, you will see why. But if you are attached to red sauce, please feel free to try the Veggie Pizza and the Four-Cheese Pizza, using one cup of our Red Sauce (page 105).

Making pizza at home is really easy to do, and once you make your first pizza you will wonder why you ever ordered out. You can make a double batch of the pizza dough and freeze it for another day. Don't be intimidated by all the specialized pizza-making equipment that you see in cookware stores: pizza stones, pizza peels, pizza cutting knives and wheels, specialized pizza pans, even pizza ovens that you put inside your own oven. I make pizza for my family in my home oven, using a rectangular baking pan. The kids love it, and my guests eat it up. In Italy, there are strict rules and regulations that govern the preparation and cooking of pizza (see "The Pizza Police," below). But in America, pizza has become so popular and has been prepared with such ingenuity for the past sixty years that I consider it an American tradition.

# The Pizza Police

Pizza originated in Naples and was popular with the poor. The most famous pizza, Pizza Margherita, is attributed to baker Raffaele Esposito, who created it in 1889 for Queen Margherita with the colors of the Italian flag: green (basil), white (mozzarella), and red (tomatoes).

Today, the True Neapolitan Pizza Association, founded in 1984 in Naples, has established strict rules that must be followed for a pizza to be declared authentic. Among these are: it must be baked in a wood-fired oven; the dough must be hand-rolled with a rolling pin, and hand-shaped; only San Marzano tomatoes can be used, and tomatoes and olive oil are layered and drizzled only in a clockwise direction. Of course, the basil leaves must be fresh.

# Homemade Pizza Crust

**Makes 2 crusts for 10 by 15-inch pizzas**

*This simple dough can be mixed by hand, in a standing mixer, or in a food processor. I use quick-rising or instant active dry yeast because it can be mixed in with the dry ingredients, which omits the extra proofing step. And I always make a double batch of dough and freeze half for up to one month. If I'm having a pizza party, I freeze several batches, thaw them, roll out and top the pizzas, and bake two at a time. You can make a plain dough or flavor it with caraway seeds, Italian herbs, or black pepper.*

3½ cups unbleached all-purpose flour, fluffed, scooped, and leveled, plus additional as needed

1 (¼-ounce) package (2¼ teaspoons) quick-rising or instant active dry yeast

2 teaspoons sugar

1 teaspoon kosher salt

1¼ cups warm water, 110°F

2 tablespoons olive oil

To mix in a bowl: In a 6-quart bowl, combine the flour, yeast, sugar, and salt. Whisk together to mix. Add the water and oil, and stir with a large spoon until a dough forms and pulls away from the sides of the bowl. Flouring your hands and adding additional flour as needed, knead the dough in the bowl until the dough is smooth and satiny, 8 to 10 minutes. Spray the top of the dough with nonstick cooking spray, cover with plastic wrap, and let rise in a warm (85°F) place until the dough has doubled, 45 to 60 minutes.

To mix in a food processor: Place the flour, yeast, sugar, and salt in the work bowl of a large-capacity (14-cup) food processor fitted with the plastic dough blade. Pulse to mix. Combine the water and oil in a measuring cup and, with the motor running, pour through the feed tube and process just until a dough forms and pulls away from the sides of the bowl. Turn out on a lightly floured surface, shape into a ball, and place in a large bowl lightly sprayed with nonstick cooking spray. Spray the top of the dough. Cover with plastic wrap and let rise until the dough has doubled, 45 to 60 minutes.

To mix in a standing mixer: Place the flour, yeast, sugar, and salt in the work bowl of a standing mixer fitted with the paddle attachment. Mix on the lowest speed for 1 minute. With the motor running, add the water and oil. Mix on low speed, stopping the machine as necessary to scrape down the sides, until the dry ingredients are fully moistened. Stop the machine, remove and scrape down the paddle, and replace with the dough hook. Knead on low speed until the dough is smooth and elastic, 8 to 10 minutes. Turn out on a lightly floured surface, shape into a ball, and place into a large bowl lightly sprayed with nonstick cooking spray. Spray the top of the dough. Cover with plastic wrap and let rise until the dough has doubled, 45 to 60 minutes.

Preheat the oven to 425°F.

When it has doubled in size, transfer the dough onto a lightly floured surface. Divide in half with a bench scraper or a sharp knife. Do not knead the dough, as that would make it hard to roll out.

On a lightly floured surface, using a rolling pin, roll out each dough half into a 10 by 15-inch rectangle. Ease and stretch the dough to fit a 10 by 15 by 1-inch (jelly roll) baking pan and spread/press the dough to the edges with lightly greased hands. Add your desired sauce and toppings for the Berghoff pizzas (see the variations). Bake for 20 to 25 minutes, until golden brown and the toppings are heated through. Cut into eight pieces to serve.

## VARIATIONS

Caraway Crust: Add 1 tablespoon of caraway seeds to the flour. Follow the remaining directions.

Herb Crust: Add 3 tablespoons of dry Italian seasoning mix to the flour. Follow the remaining directions.

Pepper Crust: Add 1 tablespoon of cracked black pepper to the flour. Follow the remaining directions.

# Freezing Pizza Dough

Yeast dough is one of the easiest foods to freeze. Once the dough is made, after the first rising, punch down the dough and knead it briefly. Cut off the amount of dough you want to freeze. Spray nonstick cooking spray inside a resealable plastic freezer bag.

Place the dough in the bag, squeeze out the excess air, seal, label and date it, and freeze. When you are ready to make your pizza, thaw the dough overnight in the refrigerator or at room temperature (4 to 6 hours). Roll out and follow the recipe as indicated.

# Berghoff Veggie Pizza

**Serves 8**

*I like veggies on my pizza but I like them uniform in size, and cooked and mellow, not big and half raw. So I created this recipe for veggie lovers. It has a lot of veggies and even meat lovers will enjoy it. I prefer the ready-to-use spinach that comes in six- or ten-ounce bags. Spinach loses volume in cooking, so if you like a little spinach, use the six-ounce bag. If you prefer a lot of spinach, go for the ten-ounce bag, but cook that in two batches.*

2 tablespoons extra-virgin olive oil

1 cup sliced yellow onion, cut ⅛ inch thick

4 cups sliced red bell pepper, stemmed, cored, cut into ⅛-inch-thick rings (about 2 large peppers)

1 (6-ounce) bag ready-to-use baby spinach, or 1 (10-ounce) bag ready-to-use spinach

½ teaspoon kosher salt

1 (10 by 15-inch) Plain or Herb Homemade Pizza Crust (page 119)

2 teaspoons minced fresh garlic

2 cups shredded mozzarella cheese

Preheat the oven to 425°F.

In a 12-inch nonstick sauté pan, heat 1 tablespoon of the oil over medium heat. Add the onion and cook, stirring, until they are tender and translucent. Add the bell pepper and cook, stirring, until they are tender and soft. Add the spinach in two batches and cook, stirring, until the spinach wilts. Sprinkle with salt. Remove the pan from the heat and let cool while you roll out the crust.

On a lightly floured surface, using a rolling pin, roll one pizza crust dough (half of the recipe) into a 10 by 15-inch rectangle. Ease and stretch to fit a 10 by 15 by 1-inch baking pan that has been sprayed with nonstick cooking spray.

In a small bowl, mix the remaining tablespoon of oil with the garlic. Scrape the mixture onto the crust and brush to cover. Spread the crust evenly with 1 cup of the cheese. Using tongs, lift the veggies from the sauté pan and distribute them evenly over the cheese. (Leave any juices in the pan.) Sprinkle with the remaining cup of cheese and bake until the crust is cooked through and the cheese is golden brown, 18 to 20 minutes.

Remove from the oven. Using a spatula, lift
and slide the pizza onto a cutting board. Cut
in half lengthwise and then each half into
quarters widthwise, into eight rectangles. Serve
immediately.

### VARIATIONS
Substitute Swiss or mild Cheddar cheese for the
mozzarella.

# Smoked Sausage and Potato Pizza

**Serves 8**

*I can't imagine not using smoked sausage and potatoes—two favorite Berghoff ingredients—on pizza. I think this is better than pepperoni pizza, and again, there is no red sauce. It's important to slice the potatoes paper thin, at most ⅛ inch thick. I do this on an inexpensive Japanese-made mandoline for the home cook.*

1 tablespoon extra-virgin olive oil

2 tablespoons brown mustard

1 (10 by 15-inch) Caraway Homemade Pizza Crust (page 121), in pan

2 cooked Thuringer or any other smoked sausage links, sliced thinly

2 unpeeled Idaho potatoes, washed and sliced ⅛ inch thick

2 cups grated regular or smoked mozzarella cheese

Preheat the oven to 425°F.

Mix the olive oil and mustard together and spread evenly over the crust. Distribute the sliced Thuringer evenly over the crust. Add the sliced potatoes evenly. Sprinkle the mozzarella on top of the potato slices. Bake until the crust is cooked through and the cheese is golden brown, 20 to 25 minutes.

Remove from the oven. Using a spatula, lift and slide the pizza onto a cutting board. Cut in half lengthwise and then each half into quarters widthwise, into eight rectangles. Serve immediately.

## THE FIRST AMERICAN PIZZERIA

The very first licensed pizzeria in America was Lombardi's, which was opened in 1905 in lower Manhattan by Neapolitan immigrant Gennaro Lombardi. The price for a whole pizza was five cents, but many customers couldn't afford a whole pie. So they offered what they could pay, say two cents, and were cut a slice that corresponded (more or less) to their price.

# Café Onion and Bacon Pizza

**Serves 8**

*This reminds me of the famous savory tart of Provence, pissaladière, which is blanketed in sweet, slowly sautéed onions. If you know in advance you'd like to make this pizza, I suggest you cook a double recipe of the Beer-Braised Onions one or two days before and refrigerate them. Those onions are versatile and good to have on hand, not just for pizza but also for adding to burgers and sandwiches and for topping grilled meats and poultry. They keep, covered and refrigerated, for up to four days.*

1 (10 by 15-inch) Caraway or Pepper Homemade Pizza Crust (page 121), in pan

1 tablespoon extra-virgin olive oil

2 tablespoons brown mustard

½ pound smoked bacon, cooked, drained and crumbled

4 cups Beer-Braised Onions (page 51)

Preheat the oven to 425°F.

Mix the oil and mustard together and brush evenly over the crust.

Distribute the bacon evenly over the crust. Spread the onions evenly over the crust. Bake until the crust is cooked through and the onions are golden and bubbly, 20 to 25 minutes.

Remove from the oven. Using a spatula, lift and slide the pizza onto a cutting board. Cut in half lengthwise and then each half into quarters widthwise, into eight rectangles. Serve immediately.

# Brat, Kraut, and Swiss Cheese Pizza with Caraway Crust

**Serves 8**

*Bratwurst, sauerkraut, and Swiss cheese do make a delicious combination when baked on a caraway crust. Be sure to squeeze the sauerkraut dry—the way you squeeze cooked spinach to remove the moisture—or the crust may become soggy. And if you are not a fan of sauerkraut, just omit it.*

2 tablespoons brown mustard

1 tablespoon extra-virgin olive oil

1 (10 by 15-inch) Caraway Homemade Pizza Crust (page 121), in pan

2 cooked bratwurst, sliced thinly

1 cup prepared sauerkraut, squeezed dry (optional)

1 cup Beer-Braised Onions (page 51)

2 cups shredded Swiss cheese

Preheat the oven to 425°F.

Mix the mustard and oil together and spread evenly over the pizza crust.

Distribute the sliced brats, sauerkraut if desired, and onions evenly on the pizza crust. Sprinkle evenly with the Swiss cheese. Bake until the crust is cooked through and the cheese is golden brown, 20 to 25 minutes.

Remove from the oven. Using a spatula, lift and slide the pizza onto a cutting board. Cut in half lengthwise and then each half into quarters widthwise, into eight rectangles. Serve immediately.

# The World's Pie

It wasn't until the 1940s that Americans suddenly went crazy for pizza. When World War II veterans came home from Italy, where they had discovered pizza, they brought the craving home. Today, 93 percent of Americans eat pizza at least once a month, and we consume twenty-three pounds per capita every year.

Americans have created gourmet pizzas, such as the Wolfgang Puck California-style with smoked salmon and caviar; and some wild ones, such as the so-called Hawaiian pizza with pineapple and ham.

Pizza is now a worldwide phenomenon and, when it comes to toppings, I think these nations take the prize:

India: pickled ginger, minced mutton, and paneer cheese

Japan: mayonnaise, potato, and bacon combo; also eel and squid

Brazil: green peas

Russia: *mockba*, a favorite combo of sardines, tuna, mackerel, salmon, and onions

Pakistan: curry

Australia: barbecued shrimp and pineapple

Costa Rica: coconut

The Netherlands: "double Dutch," a favorite combo of double cheese, double onions, and double beef

# Four-Cheese Pizza

**Serves 8**

*You will not miss the customary red sauce on this pizza. The garlic and olive oil topping is flavorful and delicious.*

1 (10 by 15-inch) Herb Homemade
Pizza Crust in pan (page 121)

1 tablespoon extra-virgin olive oil

1 tablespoon minced fresh garlic

1 cup grated Cheddar cheese

1 cup grated mozzarella cheese

½ cup grated Parmesan cheese

½ cup grated Italian fontina cheese

1 teaspoon dried oregano or
Italian herb blend (optional)

Preheat the oven to 425°F.

Brush the crust with olive oil and sprinkle with the minced garlic. Distribute the cheese and oregano, if desired, evenly over the crust. Bake until the crust is cooked through and the cheese is golden brown, 20 to 25 minutes. Remove from the oven. Using a spatula, lift and slide the pizza onto a cutting board. Cut in half lengthwise and then each half into quarters widthwise, into eight rectangles. Serve immediately.

## TO SHRED OR NOT TO SHRED

The temptation to buy already shredded cheese for pizza, sold in bags at the supermarket, can be almost overwhelming. However, I have found that it doesn't melt as well as freshly shredded cheese. By accident I discovered an alternative: When making the Beer-Cheese Soup (page 30), instead of wrapping up a chunk for me to shred, the deli at my local grocery mistakenly sliced it very, very thinly—as if for deli sandwiches. That thinly sliced cheese melted beautifully, slice by slice, in the soup. So I tried layering thinly sliced cheese on pizza. It worked very well. Just stick to the weight of the cheese as specified in the recipe. A handy guide: 4 ounces of cheese (by weight) yields ½ cup of shredded cheese; 8 ounces of cheese (by weight) yields 1 cup of shredded cheese. So if the recipe calls for 1 cup of shredded cheese, have the deli thinly slice 8 ounces or ½ pound for you.

# CHAPTER 8

# DESSERTS

# Yesterday and Today

The 1932 menu called them "pastry," but they might as well have called them "pies." There were ten pies on the menu. And the 1945 menu, which only had forty items because of World War II rationing, still had "Apple Pie." In those days, customers—especially workmen coming off the night shift—would order apple pie and coffee for their breakfast. And lemon meringue pie is still a favorite at today's Berghoff Café.

So to honor yesterday's pie tradition, I have created an easy but no less tasty version of apple pie: Apple Pie Squares with Cheddar Crust. My twist is to bake it in a 9 by 13-inch pan and slice it into squares that can be topped with an additional wedge of Cheddar. And I like to think that my recipe for Lemon Squares is just lemon pie without the meringue.

Another item that was considered dessert for decades at the Berghoff Café was coffee cake. Customers would order it for breakfast, for a midafternoon pick-me-up, and after dinner for dessert.

A sweet, tender slice of coffee cake with a cup of coffee has its own delicious logic. I remember that at home, at Grandmother Carlyn's house and at her sister's, our beloved Great-aunt Vita, there was always a pan of coffee cake. As a child, I would always pick off the streusel topping and eat it with my fingers. It must be hereditary, because today my daughter Lindsey likes the streusel topping as much as the cake. The coffee cake recipes that follow are the same kind I remember eating at the restaurant and at home.

The Berghoffs were big on cookies, not just on holidays or special occasions, but all year long. One of my all-time favorites was Great-aunt Vita's Meringue Surprises. She and her husband had no children of their own, and she made me, my sister, and our two brothers welcome for sleepovers. Sleepovers meant meringues. In those days, home ovens were heated by gas and there was always a pilot light in the oven. Great-aunt Vita would mix up her Meringue Surprises, put them on baking trays in the oven, close the oven door, and we would all go to bed. In the morning, the meringues would be perfectly baked—from the heat of the pilot light. Her other great specialty was big, soft oatmeal cookies. There were four of us and she would divide the batter into four bowls and we could each pick what we wanted to add to our cookies: raisins, chopped walnuts, or pecans, chocolate chips, or any combination. Today Great-aunt Vita's Oatmeal Cookies are still baked—and still popular—at the Berghoff Café. The Café brownie is also very much as I remember brownies baked at home: small, chocolaty, and rich. I could not end the book without including our Berghoff Bourbon–Prune Bread Pudding—and I wish you sweet dreams.

## THE WORLD'S FAIR BROWNIE

The brownie has a history older than the Berghoff Café. Food historian James Trager says the first published brownie recipe dates from 1897, which he attributes to someone's forgetting to add baking powder to a chocolate cake recipe. But, according to Chicago's Palmer House Hotel, the brownie was created by the hotel's then-chef, at the request of Bertha Honore Palmer, wife of the hotel's owner. She asked the chef to create a dessert to pack into the box lunches for the Women's Pavilion at the 1893 fair. She wanted something smaller than a wedge of cake and something that wouldn't be messy or get the ladies' hands dirty. And voilà! The brownie.

# Chocolate Brownies

**Makes 18 to 24 brownies**

*When the Berghoffs bake something chocolate, they're not kidding about the chocolate. These rich, dense brownies remind me of my childhood. I don't think they need any sauce or topping, but if you want to dress them up, just top with a dollop of lightly sweetened whipped cream.*

1 cup vegetable oil

2 cups sugar

6 eggs

1 tablespoon vanilla extract

2 cups all-purpose flour

1 cup cocoa powder

1 teaspoon baking powder

2 cups chocolate chips

1 cup toasted pecans, chopped (optional)

Lightly sweetened whipped cream, for serving

Preheat the oven to 350°F.

In a mixing bowl, combine the oil and sugar on medium speed until creamy. With the mixer running, add the eggs two at a time, until all are incorporated and the mixture is creamy. Stir in the vanilla.

In another bowl, sift together the flour, cocoa powder, and baking powder. With the mixer on low speed, add the cocoa mixture until just incorporated. Stir in the chips and nuts by hand.

Spray a 9 by 13 by 2-inch baking pan with nonstick cooking spray. Pour the batter into the baking pan and spread evenly. Bake until a wooden pick inserted into the center comes out clean, 25 to 30 minutes.

Remove from the oven and let cool on a rack to room temperature. Place the pan in the refrigerator until chilled. Cut the brownies (3 by 6) into eighteen pieces, or (4 by 6) into twenty-four. Store the brownies in an airtight container in the refrigerator.

Serve with lightly sweetened whipped cream.

# Apple Pie Squares with Cheddar Crust

**Makes twelve 3-inch squares**

*Because this crust needs to chill before being rolled out, I usually mix and refrigerate the dough the day before. Then it is fairly quick to prepare and bake the rest of the dessert the following day. This is baked in a standard 13 by 9 by 2-inch glass baking dish. The apple square pieces are large enough that one is a satisfying dessert, but small enough that you could have two without its feeling excessive.*

**CRUST**

2½ cups all-purpose flour

1 tablespoon sugar

½ teaspoon kosher salt

½ cup (1 stick) cold unsalted butter, cut into small pieces

6 tablespoons (3 ounces) vegetable shortening

1 cup shredded Cheddar cheese

⅓ to ½ cup cold water

To make the crust: Place the flour, sugar, and salt in the work bowl of a food processor fitted with a steel blade, and blend for 5 seconds. Add the butter and shortening, and pulse the processor until the mixture resembles a fine meal. Add the cheese and mix in, using four pulses of the food processor. Transfer the crust mixture to a large bowl and sprinkle 5 tablespoons of water over the dough. Use a fork to toss the mixture until moist clumps form, adding more water, 1 tablespoonful at a time, if the mixture is too dry. Gather the dough into two balls, one slightly larger, and shape each into a 6-inch flattened disk. Wrap in plastic and chill for at least 2 hours and up to 1 day before using.

To make the bottom crust, roll out the larger dough disk on a lightly floured surface to an 11 by 15-inch rectangle. Transfer the dough to an ungreased, deep 9 by 13-inch glass baking dish, patting the dough against the sides to make a short overhang all the way around.

## FILLING

⅓ to ½ cup sugar

2 tablespoons cornstarch

6 to 7 Golden Delicious apples, peeled, cored, and thinly sliced

1 tablespoon fresh lemon juice

¼ teaspoon kosher salt

2 tablespoons (1 ounce) unsalted butter, melted

1 tablespoon cold unsalted butter, cut into small pieces

Cheddar cheese triangles, for serving

Preheat the oven to 350°F.

To make the filling: In a 4-quart bowl, mix the sugar and cornstarch, then mix in the apple slices, lemon juice, and salt. Toss to coat well. Add the melted butter and stir.

Transfer the filling into the dough-lined dish and dot with the pieces of butter. Roll out the second dough disk on a lightly floured surface, to a 10 by 14-inch rectangle, and place the dough atop the filling. Press the overhang of the bottom and the top dough pieces together to seal. Trim the overhang to ½ inch. Fold the overhang under and crimp decoratively, forming a high-standing rim. Cut several small slits in the top crust to allow steam to escape. Cover with foil.

Bake the pie for 15 minutes. Remove the foil and bake until golden brown, 30 to 35 minutes. Remove from the oven and let cool on a rack for 2 to 3 hours before slicing (3 by 4) into 12 squares to serve. (For best results, let cool overnight; see Note.)

To serve, top each square with a Cheddar cheese triangle.

*Note:* This dessert may be made the day before, covered and refrigerated. Reheat in a 300°F oven until warm before serving.

# Meringue Surprises

**Makes 4 dozen cookies**

*Great-aunt Vita cooked these overnight, using the heat from the pilot in her gas oven. Today, I cook them in my home oven set at a 200°F. I line up four bowls on the counter: one for the cracked shells, one for the whites, one for breaking each egg into to make sure there is no yolk in it before I slip it into the bowl with the other whites, and one for the yolks. These meringues have only one enemy: humidity. So I don't make them on humid summer days.*

4 egg whites

¼ teaspoon cream of tartar

¼ teaspoon salt

¾ cup sugar

¾ teaspoon vanilla extract

1½ cups chocolate chips

½ cup finely chopped pecans (optional)

Preheat the oven to 200°F. Line a half sheet pan (18 by 13 inches) with parchment paper.

You will need four small bowls, preferably glass, and one large, chilled metal bowl.

Crack one egg at a time, letting the yolk drop into one bowl. If there is no yolk in the white, then slip the white into a second bowl. Repeat with all four eggs. (If you make a yolk-in-the-white mistake, just save that white for later cooking use.)

## HOW TO MEASURE PANS

Ever wonder when a recipe calls for a 9 by 13 by 2-inch pan, or a 10 by 15 by 1-inch pan, or a round 10 by 2-inch pan, how to measure? Here's how: To ascertain the length and width, use a ruler to measure the *inside* edge to *inside* edge of your pan (so you don't include the pan's thickness in your dimensions). To measure depth, place the ruler straight up from the bottom, not slanted along the sides. Use a ruler with an edge that starts with 1 true inch (no pre-zero margin). Remember that the biggest pan the standard home oven can accommodate is about 18 by 14 inches.

Pour the egg whites into the chilled metal bowl and, with an electric mixer on low speed, beat the whites until foamy. Add the cream of tartar and salt. Beat on high speed until the egg whites form soft peaks. Add the sugar, 1 tablespoon at a time, mixing on high speed. Remember to scrape the sides of the bowl. The egg white will form mountains (as Great-aunt Vita used to say). Once all the sugar is added, gently mix in the vanilla. Stir in the chocolate chips and the pecans if desired.

Drop the batter by rounded tablespoons, about 1 inch apart, onto the prepared pan.

Bake for 1½ hours. Turn off the oven. Do not open the oven door. Let the meringues rest in the residual heat for 30 additional minutes. Remove the cookie sheet from the oven. Let the meringues cool completely to room temperature. Lift them off with a thin spatula and store in large, covered tins in layers between parchment or waxed paper.

# Walnut-Applesauce Coffee Cake

**Serves 8 to10**

*This is the kind of coffee cake that my grandmother Carlyn and great-aunt Vita always had a freshly baked pan full of, so we could cut a slice. Theirs always had raisins; however, the raisins can be omitted and the cake will still be very good.*

**BATTER**

1⅔ cups all-purpose flour

1 teaspoon baking powder

½ teaspoon baking soda

Salt

½ teaspoon ground nutmeg

½ teaspoon ground ginger

½ cup vegetable oil

½ cup granulated sugar

⅓ cup brown sugar

1 large egg plus 1 large egg yolk

1 cup Applesauce (page 83)
or prepared applesauce

2 teaspoons vanilla extract

½ cup dark raisins (optional)

Preheat the oven to 350°F.

To make the batter: Sift together the flour, baking powder, baking soda, salt, and spices.

In a mixing bowl, mix the oil and sugars on medium speed until well incorporated. With the mixer running, add the egg and yolk, beating until fluffy. Stir in the applesauce, vanilla, and raisins. With the mixer on low speed, add the dry ingredients and blend, scraping down the sides and bottom of the bowl.

## EVERY DESSERT HAS ITS DAY

Among America's many national food and drink "holidays" (there is one or more for every day of the year) is April 7, National Coffee Cake Day. December 4 is National Cookie Day. December 8 is National Brownie Day. And, so as not to leave any sweet deserted, October is National Dessert Month.

## STREUSEL TOPPING

½ cup coarsely chopped toasted walnuts

½ cup all-purpose flour

¼ cup brown sugar

¼ cup (½ stick) salted butter, melted

1 teaspoon ground cinnamon

Sweetened whipped cream, for serving

Vanilla or cinnamon ice cream, for serving

Applesauce (page 83) or prepared applesauce, for serving

To make the streusel topping: In a medium-size bowl, combine all the streusel ingredients, mixing well by rubbing the mixture between your hands.

To bake the cake: Spray a 9 by 13-inch glass or metal loaf pan with nonstick cooking spray. Pour the batter in and spread evenly. Sprinkle the streusel topping evenly over the batter.

Bake until a wooden toothpick inserted in the center comes out clean, about 30 minutes.

Let cool on a rack to room temperature. Remove from the pan when cooled. Slice and serve or wrap in plastic wrap and store it in the refrigerator.

Serve with whipped cream, vanilla or cinnamon ice cream, or applesauce.

# The Chip Cookie

**Makes about 48 small or 16 large cookies**

*My kids call this "the good cookie" because they get to choose the kind of chip that goes into their respective portion.*

½ pound (2 sticks) unsalted butter, softened

1½ cups brown sugar

2 large eggs

¼ cup heavy cream

2 teaspoons vanilla extract

2½ cups all-purpose flour

1 teaspoon baking soda

½ teaspoon salt

1½ cups chips of choice: dark chocolate, milk chocolate, butterscotch, peanut butter, white chocolate, toffee

¾ cup chopped walnuts (optional)

Preheat the oven to 350°F. Line two baking sheets with parchment paper.

In a medium-size mixing bowl, cream the butter and brown sugar on medium speed until light and fluffy. Add the eggs, cream, and vanilla and continue to mix on low speed until all the ingredients are incorporated. Scrape down the bowl.

In a bowl, combine the flour, baking soda, and salt. Slowly add the dry mixture to the creamy egg mixture until incorporated. Scrape the bowl. Stir the chips and nuts into the dough by hand. Or divide the dough into three equal portions and stir ½ cup of a different kind of chip into each portion and add ¼ cup of nuts to each.

For small cookies, drop a tablespoon onto the prepared baking sheets, leaving 1 inch between cookies, and bake for 9 to 11 minutes. For large cookies, use a ¼-cup ice-cream scoop to scoop the dough onto the prepared baking sheets, leaving 2 inches between the cookies. Bake for 12 to 15 minutes, rotating the pans in the oven once midway through the baking time. Let the cookies cool slightly on the pans, then transfer them to a cooling rack. Store the cookies at room temperature in airtight containers.

# Berghoff Bourbon-Prune Bread Pudding

**Makes 8 to 10 servings**

*Prunes were very popular in the café and in our home, where they found their way into a variety of savory and sweet dishes. But this bourbon-prune bread pudding was always my favorite. It is rich, so it is not a dessert I serve often. But when I want to make something special, this is the recipe I reach for.*

10 cups cubed egg bread or challah, cut into 2-inch cubes

1½ cups good-quality pitted prunes, quartered

⅓ cup Berghoff bourbon

2 cups half-and-half

1 cup milk (use 1% or 2%, to decrease the fat)

4 large eggs plus 2 large yolks

1 cup sugar

1 teaspoon vanilla extract

¼ teaspoon almond extract

Lightly sweetened whipped cream, for serving

Vanilla or cinnamon ice cream, for serving

Caramel sauce, for serving

Spread out the bread cubes on a large baking tray and let dry, uncovered, overnight.

Preheat the oven to 350°F.

In a 1-quart bowl, combine the prunes with the bourbon; cover and let soak until the prunes are slightly plump but not all the liquid is absorbed, about 10 minutes. Strain the prune mixture, reserving the prunes and bourbon separately.

In a large bowl, whisk together the reserved bourbon, half-and-half, milk, eggs, yolks, ¾ cup of the sugar, vanilla, and almond extract until well combined.

Butter a 13 by 9 by 2-inch baking dish. Evenly distribute the bread cubes and prunes inside the baking dish. Pour the custard mixture over the bread cubes and prunes and let soak for 15 minutes, tossing once.

Meanwhile, bring about 8 cups of water to a simmer over medium-high heat.

Evenly distribute the remaining sugar over the top of the bread pudding. Set the pudding-filled baking dish into a larger roasting pan filled one-quarter of the way up with hot water. Add more hot water so it reaches a 1-inch depth along the sides of the baking dish. Bake, covered with foil, for 30 minutes. Then uncover and bake until the custard is set and the top is lightly browned, and a wooden toothpick inserted into the center comes out clean, about 15 more minutes (45 minutes in all).

Serve warm, at room temperature, or cold, topped with lightly sweetened whipped cream, vanilla or cinnamon ice cream, and caramel sauce.

## BROT PUDDING?

Old-world frugality was responsible for the creation of many Berghoff present-day desserts. For example, the great-grandfather of today's Berghoff bourbon bread pudding was the practice of recycling *Brot* (German-style black bread) and dried fruits into desserts such as bread pudding. Today's is so much better because we recycle such widely available, delicious, lighter breads as egg bread or challah, and there is no shortage of sugar, eggs, and—an ingredient Old World cooks would seldom have used for baking—premium bourbon.

# Lemon Squares

**Makes twenty 2 by 2½-inch bars**

*There are dozens of lemon bar recipes, but I believe this is one of the better ones. The crust is tender and crisp and the lemon filling is a perfect balance between sweet and puckery. In addition, these bars freeze well if stored in an airtight covered plastic container.*

## CRUST

1¾ cups all-purpose flour

¾ cup confectioners' sugar, plus additional for garnish

½ pound (2 sticks) unsalted butter, cut into chunks

## LEMON FILLING

5 large eggs

1¾ cups sugar

¾ cup fresh lemon juice

⅓ cup cake flour

1 tablespoon lemon zest

1 teaspoon baking powder

¼ teaspoon salt

Preheat the oven to 325°F. Line a 9 by 13-inch baking dish with foil and spray lightly with nonstick cooking spray.

To make the crust: In a food processor fitted with the metal blade, mix the flour and sugar. With the motor running, add the chunks of butter and process just until a dough forms. Remove the dough from the bowl (it will be crumbly) and press into an even layer into the bottom of the prepared baking dish. Bake for 20 minutes, or until lightly golden. Remove from the oven and let cool to room temperature.

To make the filling: While the crust is baking, cream together the eggs, sugar, and lemon juice with an electric mixer. Add the flour, zest, baking powder, and salt and mix until smooth. Pour over the baked crust, return to the oven, and bake until the custard is firm and thick, 20 to 25 minutes.

Remove from the oven and sprinkle with additional confectioners' sugar. Let cool on a rack completely, at least 2 to 3 hours, before cutting (4 x 5) into twenty 2 by 2½-inch bars. Or, make this a day or so in advance and refrigerate it uncut, without extra confectioners' sugar on top. It cuts easier when cold. Finish with confectioners' sugar after cutting. These freeze well for up to 1 month.

# Cream Cheese–Almond Coffee Cake

**Serves 12**

*One bite of this coffee cake takes me back to my childhood. I ate this often at the café and even more often at my grandmother Carlyn's home, where there was always a big pan of freshly baked coffee cake in the kitchen just waiting to be cut.*

## BATTER

1¼ cups granulated sugar

8 ounces cream cheese, softened

¼ pound (1 stick) unsalted butter, softened

2 large eggs

1 teaspoon vanilla extract

1 teaspoon almond extract

1⅓ cups all-purpose flour

1 teaspoon baking powder

½ teaspoon baking soda

½ teaspoon salt

¼ cup milk, at room temperature

¾ cup dried cherries

Preheat the oven to 350°F.

To prepare the batter: In a mixing bowl, combine the sugar, cream cheese, and butter on medium speed until creamy. Add the eggs and extracts, and continue to mix until creamy.

In a medium-size bowl, combine the flour, baking powder, baking soda, and salt. With the electric mixer on low speed, stir the dry ingredients into the creamy mixture just until a dough forms. Add the milk and mix until just incorporated. Stir in the dried cherries by hand.

To prepare the streusel topping: In another medium-size bowl, combine all the streusel ingredients and mix to combine.

Grease and flour a 9 by 13-inch baking pan. Pour the cake batter into the pan and spread evenly. Sprinkle the top of the cake batter evenly with the streusel topping. Bake until a wooden toothpick inserted into the center comes out clean, about 40 minutes.

## STREUSEL TOPPING

⅔ cup brown sugar

⅔ cup all-purpose flour

1 tablespoon ground cinnamon

6 tablespoons unsalted butter, softened

1 cup sliced almonds

Let the pan cool on a rack to room temperature. Remove from the pan when cooled. To serve, slice (3 by 4) into twelve pieces and serve, or wrap in plastic wrap and store in the refrigerator.

## VARIATIONS

Substitute raisins or dried cranberries for the dried cherries.

# Vita's Oatmeal Cookies

**Makes about 60 small or 21 large cookies**

*Great-aunt Vita made these cookies for my brothers and sister and me when we were kids. She would make small ones and great big ones. We always liked the big ones better. Today, Great-aunt Vita's oatmeal cookies are a favorite with customers at the Berghoff Café. For a plain and simple oatmeal-raisin cookie, omit the nuts.*

1 pound (4 sticks) unsalted butter, softened

1½ cups brown sugar, packed

2 large eggs

½ tablespoon vanilla extract

3 cups old-fashioned oatmeal

1½ cups all-purpose flour

½ tablespoon ground cinnamon

⅛ teaspoon ground nutmeg

1 teaspoon baking soda

½ teaspoon salt

1 cup dark raisins

1 cup toasted walnuts or pecans (optional)

Preheat the oven to 350°F. Line two baking sheets with parchment paper.

In a bowl, cream the butter and brown sugar with an electric mixer until light and fluffy. Add the eggs and vanilla, and continue to mix on low speed until all the ingredients are incorporated.

In a 3-quart bowl, combine the oatmeal, flour, spices, baking soda, and salt. While mixing on low speed, slowly add the flour mixture to the creamed mixture and blend until smooth. Stir in the raisins and nuts by hand.

For small cookies, scoop the dough onto the prepared baking sheets by rounded tablespoons, 1 inch apart. Or for large cookies, use a ¼-cup ice-cream scoop to scoop the dough onto the sheets, 2 inches apart. Bake the cookies until slightly golden around the edges, 12 to 14 minutes for small cookies, 14 to 16 minutes for large ones. Remove from the oven and let cool on the pans for 5 minutes before transferring with a spatula to cooling racks. Let cool to room temperature and store in airtight containers.

*Note:* You will need three large baking pans. Let one pan cool completely before adding the second batch of cookie dough. You can reuse the parchment.

**VARIATIONS**

Substitute golden raisins, currants, dried cherries, or cranberries for the dark raisins.

For a different texture, pulse the oatmeal to a finer meal in a food processor before adding to the recipe.

Omit the nuts if desired.

## COOKIES ON ICE

Some cookie doughs freeze well, for example, The Chip Cookie (page 141), and Vita's Oatmeal Cookies (page 148). I frequently make a double batch of both for two reasons: I like to freeze them in plastic containers with tight-fitting lids, so I can thaw and bake a batch of cookies another day. I also like to bring a festively wrapped container with the recipe and the proper-size cookie scoop attached, as a hostess gift. Use a container just big enough to hold the dough. Thaw overnight in the refrigerator or at room temperature for 2 to 3 hours.

# Metric Conversions and Equivalents

## METRIC CONVERSION FORMULAS

| TO CONVERT | MULTIPLY |
|---|---|
| Ounces to grams | Ounces by 28.35 |
| Pounds to kilograms | Pounds by .454 |
| Teaspoons to milliliters | Teaspoons by 4.93 |
| Tablespoons to milliliters | Tablespoons by 14.79 |
| Fluid ounces to milliliters | Fluid ounces by 29.57 |
| Cups to milliliters | Cups by 236.59 |
| Cups to liters | Cups by .236 |
| Pints to liters | Pints by .473 |
| Quarts to liters | Quarts by .946 |
| Gallons to liters | Gallons by 3.785 |
| Inches to centimeters | Inches by 2.54 |

## COMMON INGREDIENTS AND THEIR APPROXIMATE EQUIVALENTS

1 cup uncooked white rice = 185 grams
1 cup all-purpose flour = 140 grams
1 stick butter
    (4 ounces • ½ cup • 8 tablespoons) = 110 grams
1 cup butter
    (8 ounces • 2 sticks • 16 tablespoons) = 220 grams
1 cup brown sugar, firmly packed = 225 grams
1 cup granulated sugar = 200 grams

## OVEN TEMPERATURES

To convert Fahrenheit to Celsius, subtract 32 from Fahrenheit, multiply the result by 5, then divide by 9.

| DESCRIPTION | FAHRENHEIT | CELSIUS | BRITISH GAS MARK |
|---|---|---|---|
| Very cool | 200° | 95° | 0 |
| Very cool | 225° | 110° | ¼ |
| Very cool | 250° | 120° | ½ |
| Cool | 275° | 135° | 1 |
| Cool | 300° | 150° | 2 |
| Warm | 325° | 165° | 3 |
| Moderate | 350° | 175° | 4 |
| Moderately hot | 375° | 190° | 5 |
| Fairly hot | 400° | 200° | 6 |
| Hot | 425° | 220° | 7 |
| Very hot | 450° | 230° | 8 |
| Very hot | 475° | 245° | 9 |

Information compiled from a variety of sources, including *Recipes into Type* by Joan Whitman and Dolores Simon (Newton, MA: Biscuit Books, 2000); *The New Food Lover's Companion* by Sharon Tyler Herbst (Hauppauge, NY: Barron's, 1995); and *Rosemary Brown's Big Kitchen Instruction Book* (Kansas City, MO: Andrews McMeel, 1998).

## APPROXIMATE METRIC EQUIVALENTS

### VOLUME

| | |
|---|---|
| ¼ teaspoon | 1 milliliter |
| ½ teaspoon | 2.5 milliliters |
| ¾ teaspoon | 4 milliliters |
| 1 teaspoon | 5 milliliters |
| 1¼ teaspoons | 6 milliliters |
| 1½ teaspoons | 7.5 milliliters |
| 1¾ teaspoons | 8.5 milliliters |
| 2 teaspoons | 10 milliliters |
| 1 tablespoon (½ fluid ounce) | 15 milliliters |
| 2 tablespoons (1 fluid ounce) | 30 milliliters |
| ¼ cup | 60 milliliters |
| ⅓ cup | 80 milliliters |
| ½ cup (4 fluid ounces) | 120 milliliters |
| ⅔ cup | 160 milliliters |
| ¾ cup | 180 milliliters |
| 1 cup (8 fluid ounces) | 240 milliliters |
| 1¼ cups | 300 milliliters |
| 1½ cups (12 fluid ounces) | 360 milliliters |
| 1⅔ cups | 400 milliliters |
| 2 cups (1 pint) | 460 milliliters |
| 3 cups | 700 milliliters |
| 4 cups (1 quart) | 0.95 liter |
| 1 quart plus ¼ cup | 1 liter |
| 4 quarts (1 gallon) | 3.8 liters |

### WEIGHT

| | |
|---|---|
| ¼ ounce | 7 grams |
| ½ ounce | 14 grams |
| ¾ ounce | 21 grams |
| 1 ounce | 28 grams |
| 1¼ ounces | 35 grams |
| 1½ ounces | 42.5 grams |
| 1⅔ ounces | 45 grams |
| 2 ounces | 57 grams |
| 3 ounces | 85 grams |
| 4 ounces (¼ pound) | 113 grams |
| 5 ounces | 142 grams |
| 6 ounces | 170 grams |
| 7 ounces | 198 grams |
| 8 ounces (½ pound) | 227 grams |
| 16 ounces (1 pound) | 454 grams |
| 35.25 ounces (2.2 pounds) | 1 kilogram |

### LENGTH

| | |
|---|---|
| ⅛ inch | 3 millimeters |
| ¼ inch | 6 millimeters |
| ½ inch | 1¼ centimeters |
| 1 inch | 2½ centimeters |
| 2 inches | 5 centimeters |
| 2½ inches | 6 centimeters |
| 4 inches | 10 centimeters |
| 5 inches | 13 centimeters |
| 6 inches | 15¼ centimeters |
| 12 inches (1 foot) | 30 centimeters |

# Index

**A**

All-Day, All-Night Fried Egg
    Sandwich, 45
Almond Coffee Cake, Cream
    Cheese–, 146–47
Alsatian Onion Soup, 27
Anaya, Ignacio, 7
Apple Pie Squares with Cheddar
    Crust, 134–35
apples, 43
applesauce
        Applesauce, 83
        as side dish/sauce, 82
        Walnut-Applesauce Coffee
            Cake, 138–39
        Westphalian Ham Panini with
            Granny Smith Apple and
            Applesauce, 43
Asian Chicken Salad, 64
Asian Peanuts, Sweet, 9
asparagus
        Asparagus Vinaigrette, 96
        sauce for, 72

**B**

bacon
        Café Onion and Bacon Pizza,
            125
        Iceberg Wedge with Roquefort
            Dressing and Bacon, 61
        Navy Beans and Bacon, 89
        Pretzels, 19
bar. *See also* Berghoff bar
        nuts, 8–9
        panini, 37–38, 41
        salad, xvii, 60
beans
        dried, cooking, 89
        Green Beans, 88
        Navy Beans and Bacon, 89
        string, 88
Beard, James, 48, 49
beef
        chili con carne, 7, 22, 24–25
        Classic Salisbury Steak with
            Mushroom Jus Lié and
            Spaetzle, 107
        corned, xv, 37, 55

Hamburger with Beer-Braised
    Onions, 50–51
Meatballs with Red Sauce,
    104–5
beer, xiv, xv
        beer stein, history of, 11
        free lunch and, xv
        Prohibition, xv
        shot and wash, 4
        at World's Fair, 9, 22, 25, 115
*Beer: A History of Brewing in Chicago*
    (Skilnik), 4
Beer-Braised Onions, 51
Beer-Braised Onions, Hamburger
    with, 50–51
Beer-Braised Pork Loin, 114–15
Beer-Cheese Soup, 30–31
Berghoff bar
        food in, 1–2, 17
        shot and wash in, 4
Berghoff Bourbon-Prune Bread
    Pudding, 142–43
Berghoff Building, xiii, xv
Berghoff Café, xi. *See also* menu(s);
    menu, 1914; menu, 1932
        free lunch at, xv
        history of, xiv–xv
        move to Stone building, xv
        O'Hare airport, xvi, 117
        recipes from, xvii–xix
        remodel of, 117
        saloon *v.*, xiv
        simple/satisfying food of, xiii, xv
        tradition with a twist at, xvii
Berghoff, Carlyn, xi
Berghoff, Carlyn (grandmother)
        desserts and, 132, 138
        family dinners and, 14, 81, 114
        leftover bread and, 57
        recipes from, 10, 14, 83
        relish tray of, xvii, 10
        salads and, 59, 60, 61
        soup and, 21, 33
        traditional food of, xvii
        vegetables and, 81–82
Berghoff, Clement, xv
*The Berghoff Family Cookbook*, 37, 55
Berghoff Group, xv

Berghoff, Henry, 2
Berghoff, Herman Joseph, xix
        life of, xiii–xv, 2
        pretzels and, 1–2, 17
        recipes from, xvii, 37
        at World's Fair, 9, 22, 25, 115
Berghoff, Jan, 60
Berghoff, Lewis, xv, 101
Berghoff, Lindsey, 21, 132
Berghoff Restaurant, xv
Berghoff, Sarah, 21–22, 33, 69, 109
Berghoff, Todd, 21, 41
Bergo soda pop, xv
blanched vegetables, 10, 96
Blue Plate Specials, 113. *See also*
        plate lunches and dinners
        vegetarian, 109
boilermaker, 4
bourbon, Berghoff, 4
Bourbon-Basted Baked Ham, 112
bratwurst sausages, xvii, 12
        Brat and Swiss Cheese Panini, 40
        Brat, Kraut, and Swiss Cheese
            Pizza with Caraway Crust,
            127
bread
        bread crumbs, 57
        *Brot* (German-style black bread),
            143
        croutons, 57
        for panini bar, 41
        rye, 37, 46–48
Bread Pudding, Berghoff Bourbon-
    Prune, 142–43
brewery, in Indiana, xiv, 2
*Brot* (German-style black bread), 143
broth
        Homemade Chicken Broth and
            Chicken Meat, 23
        spaetzle, leftover, 85
brownies, 132
        Chocolate Brownies, 133
Buffalo Cobb, Berghoff, 63
buffet dishes
        Asparagus Vinaigrette, 96
        Carlyn's Stew du Jour with
            Vegetables, 103
        Meatballs with Red Sauce, 104–5

**C**

cabbage, 68. *See also* sauerkraut
Café Manhattan Clam Chowder, 28
Café Onion and Bacon Pizza, 125
Café Thousand Island Dressing, 78
cake. *See* coffee cake
California Dip, 11
Candied Peanuts, 9
Candied Walnuts, Pear Salad with Greens, Sun-Dried Cherries and, 71
Caper Deviled Eggs, 3
Caraway Crust, 121
Brat, Kraut, and Swiss Cheese Pizza with, 127
Caraway Pretzels, 19
"Carlyn's Ceiling Prices," 101–2
Carlyn's Stew du Jour with Vegetables, 103
Carrots, Peas and, 93
cashews, 8, 9
Cauliflower Mash, 94
celery
    Crab-Stuffed Celery, 15
    fillings, other uses for, 14
    Pimiento Cheese-Stuffed Celery, 14
    Smoked Gouda and Dried Tomato–Stuffed Celery, 15
Champagne Vinaigrette, 73
Champion, Charles, 42
Cheddar Crust, Apple Pie Squares with, 134–35
cheese. *See also* pizza; *specific cheeses*
    Beer-Cheese Soup, 30–31
    Brat and Swiss Cheese Panini, 40
    Cheese Pretzels, 19
    for panini bar, 41
    on pie, 131
    Pimiento Cheese Panini, 39
    Pimiento Cheese-Stuffed Celery, 14
    processed, 42
    sandwiches, 37, 42
    sliced *v.* shredded, 129
Cherries, Sun-Dried, Pear Salad with Greens, Candied Walnuts, and, 71
chicken(s), 114
    Asian Chicken Salad, 64
    Berghoff Buffalo Cobb, 63
    Grilled Chicken Breast, 65
    Homemade Chicken Broth and Chicken Meat, 23
    Homemade Chicken Spaetzle Soup, 29
    leftover, uses for, 29, 63, 64
chili con carne

Chili con Carne, 24–25
    history of, 25
    in nachos, 7, 24
    at World's Fair, 1893, 22, 24, 25
chili powder, 25
"chili queens," 25
The Chip Cookie, 141
Chocolate Brownies, 133
chocolate chip cookie, xvii, 141
Chocolate Chip Pretzels, 19
Church, Bruce, 61
Cinnamon-Raisin Pretzels, 19
Clam Chowder, Café Manhattan, 28
Classic Salisbury Steak with Mushroom Jus Lié and Spaetzle, 107
club house sandwiches, 48
Club House Sandwich, 49
cocktail party menu, 2
coffee cake, 131–32
    Cream Cheese–Almond Coffee Cake, 146–47
    Streusel Topping, 139, 147
    Walnut-Applesauce Coffee Cake, 138–39
cold potatoes, reviving, 98
Coleslaw, 68
Columbian Exposition, 9, 24, 25, 115. *See also* World's Fair
cookies, 132
    The Chip Cookie, 141
    chocolate chip, xvii, 141
    double batches/freezing/ thawing dough, 149
    Meringue Surprises, 136–37
    Vita's Oatmeal Cookies, 148–49
corn
    Berghoff Buffalo Cobb, 63
    popcorn, 30
corned beef sandwiches, xv, 37
Corned Beef Sandwich, 55
crab patty melt, 15
Crab-Stuffed Celery, 15
cracker crumbs, homemade, 109
Cracker Jack, 9
cream cheese, pimiento, 14
Cream Cheese–Almond Coffee Cake, 146–47
Creole seasoning mixes, 34
crisphead lettuce, 61
croutons, 57
crudités, 10
    dips for, 3, 11, 73
Crum, George, 38
Culinary Institute of America, 81
customers' favorites, xix

**D**

daily specials, 101–2. *See also* plate lunches and dinners
Day-After-Thanksgiving Soup, 35
desserts, xix, 131–32. *See also* brownies; coffee cake; cookies; pie
    Apple Pie Squares with Cheddar Crust, 134–35
    Berghoff Bourbon-Prune Bread Pudding, 142–43
    bread crumbs in, 57
    Lemon Squares, 144
    national holidays, 138
    sauces for, 82
Deviled Eggs with Three Fillings, 3–5
Dill, New Potato Salad with, 69
dips
    California, 11
    for crudités, 3, 11, 73
    Green Onion Dip, 11
double batches
    cookie dough, 149
    onions, 51, 125
    pizza dough, 118, 119, 121
    red sauce, 105
    soups, 22
double duty salad dressings, 73

**E**

eggs
    All-Day, All-Night Fried Egg Sandwich, 45
    Deviled Eggs with Three Fillings, 3–5
    hard-boiled, 5
    in spaetzle, 82, 85
Esposito, Raffaele, 118

**F**

Fahrenheit, converting to Celsius, 150
family dinners, 103, 114. *See also* Sunday dinners
fennel seeds, 114
fillings
    celery, other uses for, 14
    deviled egg, other uses for, 3
    Deviled Eggs with Three Fillings, 3–5
    for panini, 3, 14, 41
fish
    for panini bar, 41
    Smoked Salmon Deviled Eggs, 4
"flame tamers," 115
flavor boosters, for soups, 32
Four-Cheese Pizza, 129
frankfurters, xv, xix, 37
The Real Thing Frankfurter, 57

free lunch, xv
free nuts, 8
freezing
    cookie dough, 149
    pizza dough, 118, 119, 121
    soups, 22
French dressings
    Today's French Dressing, 77
    Yesterday's French Dressing, 76
Fresh Baked Pretzels, 17–19
Fresh Express, 61
Fromage de Brie, 37, 43
frugality, Old World, 143
fruit, sauces for, 73

**G**

Gebhardt, William, 25
Gouda, Smoked, and Dried Tomato–
    Stuffed Celery, 15
Great Depression, 101, 113
Green Beans, 88
green onions, 11, 82
Green Onion Dip, 11
Grilled Chicken Breast, 65

**H**

ham
    boiled ham sandwich, xv, 37
    Bourbon-Basted Baked Ham,
        112
    Westphalian Ham Panini with
        Granny Smith Apple and
        Applesauce, 43
Hamburger with Beer-Braised
    Onions, 50–51
hard-boiled eggs, 5
heat diffusers, 115
herbs
    caraway seeds, 19, 121, 127
    dill, 69
    fennel seeds, 114
    Herb Crust, 121
    New Potato Salad with Dill, 69
    in pizza crust, xvii, 118, 121
    in salad dressing, 77
    with spaetzle, 82, 86
Hertenstein, Karl, 95
holidays
    Day-After-Thanksgiving Soup,
        35
    national, for desserts, 138
Homemade Chicken Broth and
    Chicken Meat, 23
Homemade Chicken Spaetzle Soup,
    29
homemade cracker crumbs, 109
Homemade Pizza Crust, 119–21
Horseradish Deviled Eggs, 5

**I**

iceberg lettuce, 59, 61
Iceberg Wedge with Roquefort
    Dressing and Bacon, 61
ingredients, xvi
    common, and equivalents, 150
    quantity buying, 101
    reusing, recycling and
        reinventing, xvi–xvii, 22,
        143

**K**

Kraft, James L., 42

**L**

leeks, 31
leftovers
    bread, 57
    chicken, uses for, 29, 63, 64
    cooking liquid, from mashed
        potatoes, 99
    meat loaf, 110
    in sandwiches, xvii, 110, 115
    spaetzle broth, 85
    turkey, uses for, 34, 35
    vegetables, 35, 98
lemon juice, 96
Lemon Squares, 144
lettuce, 59, 61
Lipton Onion Soup mix, 11
Lombardi, Gennaro, 124
Lombardi's, 124
Lyonnaise Potatoes, 91–92

**M**

make-ahead salads, 74
Margherita, Queen, 118
mashed potatoes, xvii, 81–82
    cooking liquid from, leftover, 99
    Mashed Potatoes, 99
mashes, vegetable, 82
    Cauliflower Mash, 94
    Sweet Potato Mash, 98
mayonnaise, 68
measurements
    metric conversions and
        equivalents, 150
    pans, measuring, 136
meat, for panini bar, 41
Meat Loaf, Turkey, 110
Meatballs with Red Sauce, 104–5
menu(s), xv–xix
    1945, 101–2, 131
    1986, 60
    history of, xv
    tailgate or cocktail party, 2
menu, 1914
    prices, xv, 22

relish section, 10
salads, 59, 68
sandwiches, 37, 38, 39, 43
soups, 22, 24
menu, 1932
    desserts, 131
    lettuce salad, 59
    mushroom sauce, 95
    plate dinners, 95, 102
    prices, 95, 102
    relish section, 10
Meringue Surprises, 136–37
meringues, 132
metric conversions and equivalents,
    150
Mini-Pretzels, 19
Moon's Lake House resort, 38
mushrooms
    Classic Salisbury Steak with
        Mushroom Jus Lié and
        Spaetzle, 107
    sauce, 95
    Sautéed Mushrooms Jus Lié, 95

**N**

nachos
    Berghoff, 7
    chili con carne in, 7, 24
    history of, 7
naked sandwiches, 38
Navy Beans and Bacon, 89
near beer, xv
New England–style v. Manhattan
    clam chowder, 28
New Potato Salad with Dill, 69
noodles. *See also* pasta, sauces for
    Asian Chicken Salad, 64
    Homemade Chicken Spaetzle
        Soup, 29
    soba, 64
NOW (National Organization for
    Women), xiv
nuts, bar, 8–9. *See also specific nuts*

**O**

Oatmeal Cookies, Vita's, 148–49
O'Hare airport, xvi, 117
Okra, Turkey, and Rice Soup, 34–35
onions
    Alsatian Onion Soup, 27
    Beer-Braised Onions, 51
    Café Onion and Bacon Pizza,
        125
    double batches, 51, 125
    green, 11, 82
    Hamburger with Beer-Braised
        Onions, 50–51
    kinds of, 82

Lipton Onion Soup mix, 11
sweet, 82
open-face sandwiches, 38
oven temperatures, 150

**P**
Palmer, Bertha Honore, 132
Palmer building, xv
Palmer House Hotel, 132
Palmer, Potter, xv
panini, 37–38
    bar, 37–38, 41
    Brat and Swiss Cheese Panini, 40
    fillings for, 3, 14, 41
    history of, 42
    Pimiento Cheese Panini, 39
    spreads for, 41, 73
    Westphalian Ham Panini with Granny Smith Apple and Applesauce, 43
pans, measuring, 136
pasta, sauces for, 73
pastry bag, disposable, 14
patty melt, crab, 15
Peanut Butter Dressing, 75
peanuts, 8–9
    Candied Peanuts, 9
    at Chicago World's Fair, 9
    Savory Spicy Peanuts, 8
    Sweet and Spicy Peanuts, 9
    Sweet Asian Peanuts, 9
Pear Salad with Greens, Candied Walnuts, and Sun-Dried Cherries, 71
Peas and Carrots, 93
Pendery, DeWitt Clinton, 25
Pepper Crust, 121
pepper sauce, red, 25
pie, 131
Apple Pie Squares with Cheddar Crust, 134–35
Pimiento Cheese Panini, 39
Pimiento Cheese-Stuffed Celery, 14
*pissaladière* (savory tart), 125
pistachios, 8, 9
pizza, xvii, 117–18
    Brat, Kraut, and Swiss Cheese Pizza with Caraway Crust, 127
    Café Onion and Bacon Pizza, 125
    Four-Cheese Pizza, 129
    Italian rules for, 118
    sauce on, xvii, 117–18
    sliced v. shredded cheese on, 129
    Smoked Sausage and Potato Pizza, 124

toppings, xvii, 128
Veggie Pizza, Berghoff, 122–23
pizza crusts, xvii, 118
    Caraway, 121
    herbs in, xvii, 118, 121
    Homemade Pizza Crust, 119–21
    Pepper, 121
pizza dough
    double batch/freezing, 118, 119, 121
    thawing, 121
pizzeria, first American, 124
plate lunches and dinners, 95, 101–2, 102
    Beer-Braised Pork Loin, 114–15
    Bourbon-Basted Baked Ham, 112
    Carlyn's Stew du Jour with Vegetables, 103
    Classic Salisbury Steak with Mushroom Jus Lié and Spaetzle, 107
    how to arrange on plate, 107
    Meatballs with Red Sauce, 104–5
    Schnitzels, 108–9
    Turkey Meat Loaf, 110
    vegetarian, 109
Plato, xvi
popcorn, 30
pork. *See also* ham
    Beer-Braised Pork Loin, 114–15
    Schnitzels, 108–9
"pot watchers," 115
potato chips, xvii, 38
potatoes, xvi
    Lyonnaise Potatoes, 91–92
    mashed, xvii, 81–82, 99
    New Potato Salad with Dill, 69
    Potato Soup, 33
    reviving cold, 98
    Smoked Sausage and Potato Pizza, 124
    Sweet Potato Mash, 98
poultry, 114. *See also* chicken; turkey
    for panini bar, 41
    Schnitzels, 108–9
pretiolas ("little rewards"), 18
pretzels, xvii–xix
    Bacon, 19
    in Berghoff history, 1–2, 17
    boiling, 17
    Caraway, 19
    Cheese, 19
    Chocolate Chip, 19
    Cinnamon-Raisin, 19
    Fresh Baked Pretzels, 17–19
    history of, 18

Mini-, 19
shaping, 18–19
soft v. hard, 18
prices, menu, xv, 22, 95, 101–2
Prohibition, xv
Prune Bread Pudding, Berghoff Bourbon-, 142–43
Puck, Wolfgang, 128

**R**
Raisin, Cinnamon-, Pretzels, 19
Ranch dressing, 79
The Real Thing Frankfurter, 57
red pepper sauce, 25
Red Sauce, 105
Red Sauce, Meatballs with, 104–5
red wine vinegar, 76
Reichel, Matt
    sandwiches and, 38, 49, 51, 56
    soup and, 22, 28, 34
relish tray, xvii
Berghoff Relish Tray, 10
    Reuben, Turkey, 52–53
    reusing, recycling, and reinventing ingredients, xvi–xvii, 22, 143. *See also* leftovers
    Rice, Turkey, Okra and, Soup, 34–35
    Roasted Herb-Marinated Turkey Breast, 54
    roasts, 38
    Roquefort Cheese Dressing, 72
    Roquefort Dressing and Bacon, Iceberg Wedge with, 61
    Rueckheim, Frederick William, 9
    rye bread, 37
    Berghoff Sandwich Rye, 46–48
    sauerkraut rye, 47
rye flour, 48

**S**
salad dressings, 60
    Café Thousand Island Dressing, 78
    Champagne Vinaigrette, 73
    double duty, 73
    green vegetables, acid and, 96
    herbs in, 77
    Peanut Butter Dressing, 75
    Ranch, 79
    Roquefort Cheese Dressing, 72
    Roquefort Dressing and Bacon, Iceberg Wedge with, 61
    as spreads, 73
    Thousand Island Dressing, Shrimp Salad with, 66–67
    Today's French Dressing, 77

Yesterday's French Dressing, 76
salads, xix, 59–60
    Asian Chicken Salad, 64
    bar, xvii, 60
    Buffalo Cobb, Berghoff, 63
    Coleslaw, 68
    Iceberg Wedge with Roquefort
        Dressing and Bacon, 61
    make-ahead, 74
    New Potato Salad with Dill, 69
    Pear Salad with Greens,
        Candied Walnuts, and
        Sun-Dried Cherries, 71
    Shrimp Salad with Thousand
        Island Dressing, 66–67
    vegetarian, 61, 69
Salisbury, James H., 107
Salisbury Steak with Mushroom Jus
    Lié and Spaetzle, Classic, 107
Salmon, Smoked, Deviled Eggs, 4
Sandwich Rye, Berghoff, 46–48
sandwiches, xv, xix, 37–38. *See also*
    panini
    All-Day, All-Night Fried Egg
        Sandwich, 45
    boiled ham, xv, 37
    cheese, 37, 42
    club house, 48, 49
    corned beef, xv, 37, 55
    Hamburger with Beer-Braised
        Onions, 50–51
    leftovers in, xvii, 110, 115
    naked, 38
    open-face, 38
    potato chips inside, xvii, 38
    The Real Thing Frankfurter, 57
    Sub, Berghoff, 56
    Turkey Reuben, 52–53
Sta Marie, Enrique "Bong," 46
Saratoga Chips, 38
Saratoga Club-House, 48
sauces. *See also* applesauce
    for asparagus, 72
    for desserts, 82
    for fruit, 73
    mushroom, 95
    on pizzas, xvii, 117–18
    Red, 105
    red pepper, 25
    Red Sauce, Meatballs with,
        104–5
    salad dressings as, 73
    for vegetables, 73, 81
sauerkraut, xi, xvii, 52
    Brat, Kraut, and Swiss Cheese
        Pizza with Caraway Crust,
        127
    rye bread, 47

Turkey Reuben, 52–53
sausages
    bratwurst, xvii, 12, 40, 127
    Sausage Wellingtons, 12–13
    Smoked Sausage and Potato
        Pizza, 124
Sautéed Mushrooms Jus Lié, 95
Savory Spicy Peanuts, 8
scallions, 82
Schnitzels, 108–9
shot and wash, 4
Shrimp Salad with Thousand Island
    Dressing, 66–67
shrimp, thawing, 66
side dishes, 81–82
    applesauce, 82, 83
    Asparagus Vinaigrette, 96
    Cauliflower Mash, 94
    Green Beans, 88
    Lyonnaise Potatoes, 91–92
    Mashed Potatoes, 99
    Navy Beans and Bacon, 89
    Peas and Carrots, 93
    Sautéed Mushrooms Jus Lié, 95
    Spaetzle, Berghoff, 85–86
    Sweet Potato Mash, 98
"simmer rings," 115
Skilnik, Bob, 4
Smoked Gouda and Dried Tomato–
    Stuffed Celery, 15
Smoked Salmon Deviled Eggs, 4
Smoked Sausage and Potato Pizza,
    124
soba noodles, 64
soda pop, Bergo, xv
soups, xix, 21–22. *See also* chili con
    carne
    Alsatian Onion Soup, 27
    Beer-Cheese Soup, 30–31
    Café Manhattan Clam
        Chowder, 28
    cooking liquid from mashed
        potatoes in, 99
    Day-After-Thanksgiving Soup,
        35
    double batches/freezing, 22
    flavor boosters for, 32
    Homemade Chicken Broth and
        Chicken Meat, 23
    Homemade Chicken Spaetzle
        Soup, 29
    leftover spaetzle broth in, 85
    Lipton Onion Soup mix, 11
    Potato Soup, 33
    Turkey, Okra, and Rice Soup,
        34–35
    vegetarian, 27, 33
spaetzle, 87

Berghoff Spaetzle, 85–86
    eggs in, 82, 85
    Homemade Chicken Spaetzle
        Soup, 29
spinach, 122
sporting event-theme party menu, 2
spreads
    for panini, 41, 73
    salad dressings as, 73
*Steinkrug* (stone mug), 11
stew, 25, 107
Stew du Jour with Vegetables,
    Carlyn's, 103
Stone building, xv
Stone, Horatio O., xv
stoves, gas and electric, 115
Streusel Topping, 139, 147
string beans, 88
Stuffed Celery Three Ways, 14–15
Sturgis, Julius, 18
Sub, Berghoff, 56
Sunday dinners, 14, 38, 81
Sweet and Spicy Peanuts, 9
Sweet Asian Peanuts, 9
sweet onions, 82
Sweet Potato Mash, 98
sweet vinaigrette, 60
swiss cheese
    Brat and Swiss Cheese Panini,
        40
    Brat, Kraut, and Swiss Cheese
        Pizza with Caraway Crust,
        127

**T**
tailgate menu, 2
Tappendon, William, 38
Texas Lavanderas, 25
thawing
    cookie dough, 149
    pizza dough, 121
    shrimp, 66
Thousand Island Dressing, Café, 78
Thousand Island Dressing, Shrimp
    Salad with, 66–67
Today's French Dressing, 77
Tomato-Stuffed Celery, Dried,
    Smoked Gouda and, 15
toppings
    pizza, xvii, 128
    Streusel, 139, 147
tradition with a twist, xvii
Trager, James, 132
turkey
    Club House Sandwich, 49
    leftover, uses for, xvi, 34–35
    Roasted Herb-Marinated Turkey
        Breast, 54

Turkey Meat Loaf, 110
Turkey, Okra, and Rice Soup,
34–35
Turkey Reuben, 52–53

**U**
updated dishes, xvii

**V**
veal, 108
vegetables, 81–82. *See also* crudités;
    relish tray; *specific vegetables*
    acid, salad dressings and, 96
    blanched, 10, 96
    Carlyn's Stew du Jour with
        Vegetables, 103
    leftovers, 35, 98
    mashes, 82, 94, 98
    Peas and Carrots, 93
    sauces for, 73, 81

vegetarian dishes
    Blue Plate Specials, 109
    green beans, 88
    salads, 61, 69
    soups, 27, 33
Veggie Pizza, Berghoff, 122–23
Victory Club restaurant, 7
vinaigrette
    Asparagus Vinaigrette, 96
    Champagne, 73
    sweet, 60
vinegar, 76, 96
Vita, Great-aunt, 132, 136, 138, 148
Vita's Oatmeal Cookies, 148–49

**W**
Walnut-Applesauce Coffee Cake,
    138–39
Walnuts, Candied, Pear Salad with
    Greens, Sun-Dried Cherries and,
    71
water, impurity of, 4
Wellingtons, Sausage, 12–13
Westphalian Ham Panini with Granny
    Smith Apple and Applesauce, 43
whiskey, xv, 4
World War I, 42
World War II, 101, 117, 128, 131
World's Fair
    Chicago, 1893, 9, 22, 24, 25,
        115, 132
    London, 1851, 115

**Y**
Yesterday's French Dressing, 76